SHI'A ISLAM:
FROM RELIGION TO REVOLUTION

Shi'a Islam: From Religion to Revolution

BY HEINZ HALM

translated from the German by Allison Brown

Markus Wiener Publishers
Princeton

For information write to: Markus Wiener Publishers
114 Jefferson Road, Princeton, NJ 08540

Library of Congress Cataloging-in-Publication Data

Halm, Heinz, 1942–
    [Schiitische Islam. English]
    Shi'a Islam: from religion to revolution/by Heinz Halm:
translated from German by Allison Brown.
    (Princeton Series on the Middle East)
    Includes bibliographical references and index.
    ISBN 1-55876-134-9 hardcover
    ISBN 1-55876-135-7 paperback
    1. Shi'a—History.   I. Title.   II. Series
BP192.H3513   1996
297'.82—dc20   96-35459
                                                            CIP

Printed in the United States of America on acid-free paper.

Table of Contents

PART ONE
The House of Sorrow
The Twelve Imams

PART TWO
The Deluge of Weeping
Flagellant Procession and Passion Play

PART THREE
The Government of the Expert
The Islam of the Mullahs

Preface

Twenty years ago, surely, there was hardly an American or European who had ever heard the word *Ayatollah*, and most likely only very few could even make heads or tails of the word *Shi'a*. Not until October 1978 did the existence of Shi'i Muslims make an impression upon our consciousnesses. At that time, namely, television pictures of the Iranian revolutionary Âyatollâh Khomeinî flooded our living rooms every evening. He had been expelled from Iraq and had settled in Neauphle-le-Château near Paris to take up the struggle against the Shah from there. The image of the Shi'ites and Shi'ism in the Western media is thus—as could only be expected—essentially influenced by the events of the Iranian revolution and political developments of the Islamic Republic of Iran, which, immediately upon its founding, sought conflict with the West. Shi'ites soon became involved in other conflicts in the Middle East: the civil war in Lebanon, when Lebanese Shi'ites entered the military conflict following the Israeli invasion in 1982; the civil war in Afghanistan, in which Shi'i *mujâhidîn* also participated; the conflict surrounding Nagorno-Karabakh between Christian Armenians and Shi'i Azeris; and the revolt of the Shi'ites in southern Iraq against Saddam Hussein after the second war in the Persian Gulf in March 1991. Of course, Shi'ites were only mentioned in news reports when they offered real *news*, that is, as revolutionaries or civil war fighters, kidnappers or terrorists.

Most people understood very little of the religious beliefs of the Shi'ites and their more than thirteen-century-old tradition. At best there were pictures of flagellants, scourging their backs till they bled or beating their brows with swords. The mutillating images suggested something totally foreign and incomprehensible, something that could only be described as "mystical" or "irrational." Shi'ism appeared to be an especially threatening form of Islam, which had the notorious label of fanatic in any case. Particularly shrouded were the connections between the religion and revolutionary emergence of the Shi'a, even though such a connection was generally implied as given: In Iran, *Shi'i Islam* had started a revolution, and not Iranians who happened to be Shi'ites. Was that the case? Is Shi'i Islam revolutionary *per se,* and are Shi'i Muslims in fact 120 million potential revolutionaries?

The demonization of the Shi'a, which, at the height of the Iranian revolution, was a matter of course in the West, has since dispelled to some extent. The revolt of Iraqi Shi'ites against Saddam Hussein even served for a while to blur the traditional distinctive images of friend and foe in the media, even if Western politicians and commentators soon resumed their familiar, vague fear of Shi'i expansion: the image of a weakened Saddam who held Iraq together was still preferred over that of an Iranian-dominated Shi'i state in southern Iraq.

This book is about neither the Iranian revolution nor Middle East politics in general, but the religion of the Shi'ites. Since religion and politics are so closely intertwined in the Middle East, however, it is inevitable that political events continue to slip into the foreground. Of course, the Iranian revolution is also a part of the history of Shi'i Islam and, conversely, events in Iran cannot be understood without knowledge of Shi'ism. The revolution itself served to transform Shi'ism, and it is these processes of change that are the actual subject of this book.

Shi'ism is as old as Islam itself. Followers of Shi'ism were always in a minority and usually the opposition; they were sometimes persecuted, despised, and oppressed. The history of Shi'ism has had a lasting impact on its worldview and its attitude to politics and society; this attitude in turn can be seen in present-day political conflicts.

Shi'ism first developed in Iraq, which today is still one of the core countries of Shi'i Islam. The decisive events of the Shi'a passion history took place in Iraq; here are the mausoleums of six of the twelve imams, and this is where Shi'i theology developed in the Middle Ages. Shi'ism is thus originally an Arabic phenomenon, as is Islam itself, and a large majority of its literature has been written in Arabic, even by Iranian authors. Arabic is still the language used by Shi'i theologians worldwide. More than half of all Iraqis are members of the Shi'a faith; they live predominantly in the southern part of the country (about 10 million).

The first Shi'a settlement in Iran, the Arabic colony of Qom, was already founded in the eighth century, but the Shi'ites long remained a minority. Their communities were concentrated in the cities of northwestern Iran. A systematic policy of Shi'ization was not introduced until a Shi'i Shah Dynasty was established in 1501; this process was concluded around the end of the seventeenth century. The Turkish-speaking population in Azerbaijan was also affected by this policy. More than five million Azeris in the now independent, former Soviet republic of Azerbaijan (three-quarters of the total population) and twelve million Azeris in the Azerbaijan province in northern Iran are Shi'ites. The Islamic country with the largest proportion of Shi'ites is Iran, where they comprise 91% of the total population (approx. 53 million). Shi'i communities in South Lebanon and in the Lebanese Beqâ'a valley were founded as early as the tenth century. Today they are the largest religious group in terms of numbers in the country (more than one million). There are also Shi'ites in the Arabic states west of the Persian Gulf, in Saudi Arabia and the smaller gulf nations (approx. 1 million combined). The Mongolian Hezâra in the central mountains of Afghanistan are Shi'i Muslims (approx. 2 million) and on the Indian subcontinent, there are larger islands of predominantly Shi'i populations in the Pakistani Punjab (approx. 5.5 million); other Shi'i populations exist in India, around Avadh (Oudh) north of the Ganges and around Hyderabad in the central

Deccan peninsula, as well as the Kashmir region disputed by India and Pakistan (together approx. 23 million). In all, there are approximately 100 million Shi'ites in the Islamic core countries, and about 110 million if the Shi'i diaspora is included, making up about 10% of all Muslims worldwide.

Shi'i settlements are spread out, forming no contiguous territory, and Shi'i Muslims belong to various ethnic-linguistic groups: they are Arabs, Iranians, Turkish Azeris, Mongolian Hezâra, and Indians.

When *Shi'ites* are mentioned in the following, the "Imamites" or "Twelvers" are meant, whose involvement in political events put them in the headlines in the last few years. Smaller Shi'i denominations such as the Isma'ilis (Seveners) of the Agha Khan, the Indian Bohras, the Yemenite Zaydis (Fivers), the Syrian Nusayri-Alawis, or the Druze shall not be considered here (for information on these see my book, *Shiism*, Edinburgh 1991, which provides a survey of Shi'ism as a whole).

The focus of the following presentation will be the passion play rituals, which comprise the true core of religious observance of Twelver Shi'ism and provide a necessary key in gaining access to an understanding of Twelver Shi'ism's essential ideas of faith. The Islam of the Shi'a is a religion like any other; and as revolutionaries, Shi'ites are to be judged as any other revolutionaries. As a party involved in the conflicts in the conflict-laden Middle East, they are one group among many. The aim of this book is not to compensate for the widespread negative image of the Shi'a with an idealized view, but rather to replace it with accurate information.

Remarks on the spelling
of Arabic and Persian words and names

The twenty German consonant phonemes are no comparison with the large number of consonants in Arabic (28), [compared with 30 consonant phonemes in English—trans.]. Iranians, who speak an Indo-European language, correctly write the vast number of words borrowed from Arabic, but even they have difficulty pronouncing a number of Arabic sounds. This book has not used a scholarly transliteration of the words and names from the two Oriental languages. In order to provide at least a hint as to the correct pronunciation, a spelling convention has been chosen with the English-speaking reader in mind. The only sign added is the circumflex to indicate long vowel sounds, which are usually stressed. The Arabic consonants *hamza* and *'ayn* are both represented by an apostrophe, although only the former indicates a glottal stop. The following conventions that have developed based on the transliteration commonly used in English-language publications have been used here:

th   corresponds to the voiceless th in Engl. *thing*
dh   corresponds to the voiced th in *this*
kh   is a "hard" h, corresponding approximately to the German ch in *Bach* (velar fricative)
q   is a "dull" k-sound, formed at the back of the soft palate (velar)
r   is an r formed with the tip of the tongue
gh   is an uvular r
h   is a voiced consonant, even at the end of a syllable, e.g., in *Mahdî*

s   is always voiceless, e.g., in *al-Hasan* or *al-Husayn*

z   is a voiced s, corresponding to the English z

The spelling of the names in the travelogues cited in the second part of the book have been maintained as in the originals. In some segments translated from German or French, adaptations have been made for English-language readers.

PART ONE

The House of Sorrow
The Twelve Imams

1. The Commander of the Faithful: Alî ibn Abî Tâlib (656-661)

On his return to Medina from his final pilgrimage to Mecca in the year 632, Muhammad the Prophet and his caravan rested at the pool of Khumm, approximately halfway between the two cities. On March 16, the following is said to have taken place, an exchange still celebrated today by the Shi'ites: "Am I not more appropriate for authority over you than yourselves?" When the community joyfully answered yes, Muhammad continued, "Whomsoever I am the authority over, 'Alî is also the authority over."

The two statements by the Prophet are ambiguous in the original Arabic. They have been translated here as they are understood by the Shi'ites. A Shi'i commentator explained: "Thus he (the Prophet) required for him ('Alî), through laying down obedience to him and his authority (over them), the same authority as he had over them, and which he made them acknowledge and which they did not deny. This is clear (evidence) of the nomination of him for the Imamate and for succession to his position."[1]

The Arabic word *imâm* means "leader of the community"; it is formed from the same root as the word for "community" *(umma)*. *Khalîfa,* on the other hand, means "representative" or "successor." According to the Shi'i interpretation of the events at the pool of Khumm, the Prophet, who knew his end was near, declared Alî to be his successor as leader of the Islamic community.

Alî ibn Abî Tâlib was Muhammad's cousin, son of his uncle, Abû Tâlib. Muhammad, orphaned at an early age, had been taken into his uncle's home and raised there. Later, when the uncle himself became impoverished, Muhammad took his young cousin Alî into his own household to relieve his uncle's burden. Alî was supposedly the first—after Muhammad's first wife Khadîja—to accept the Prophet's message. When Muhammad was forced to leave his hometown of Mecca in the year 622 and settle in Medina, Alî followed shortly afterward. According to Shi'i tradition, Alî assured the Prophet's safe flight from Mecca by sleeping in Muhammad's bed wearing his clothing, so that the Meccans who forced their way into the Prophet's bedchamber to kill him were surprised to find the wrong person there and their plan foiled.

During his ten years in Medina (622-632), Muhammad laid the groundwork for an Islamic state. His cousin was his closest confidant, becoming his son-in-law as well by marrying Muhammad's daughter Fâtima. When the Prophet entered the conquered Mecca in 630, Alî—according to Shi'i tradition—carried the banner. It was Alî who captured Yemen and converted its people to Islam, and when the Prophet set out on his final battle against the oasis city of Tabûk in northern Arabia (autumn 630), it was Alî whom he appointed as his representative *(khalîfa)* in Medina.

When the Prophet died on June 8, 632, however, it was not Alî who was named his successor, but Muhammad's old companion Abû Bakr, who had accompanied him on his journey into exile *(hijra)* to Medina. Abû Bakr died after serving only two years as caliph; he is said to have named Umar, another companion of Muhammad, to be his successor. The military expansion of the Arabian Empire in the name of Islam began during Umar's ten-year caliphate (634-644)—at the cost of the two major powers at the time, the Byzantine Empire and the Persian Empire of the Sassanians. Within only a few years, Palestine and Syria, Egypt and Mesopotamia (Arabic *al-Irâq)* were conquered.

After Umar's death, a six-member council *(shûrâ)* convened to elect a new caliph. They chose Uthmân of the Meccan Umayyad clan. Alî, as one of the most influential companions of the Prophet, was also one of the members of the council. He was 46 years old at the time (born in 598). Alî did not challenge the election of Uthmân, though he was clearly in the opposition. The contrast between the two men was reflected in tensions which soon triggered a bloody conflict that divided the original

Muslim community. Uthmân, who was also an outstanding war comrade of the Prophet, represented the Umayyad clan, the established urban aristocracy of Mecca, which long remained heathen—certainly a bone of contention for the Prophet. They had since accepted Islam—albeit as an act of expediency—and now they set out once again to regain their previous supremacy within the framework of the new Islamic community. Alî, on the other hand, represented the first Muslims, the exiles from Medina, the original religious nobility, so to speak, whose merits were the early acceptance of Islam and the hijra, the voluntary exile in Medina.

Tensions within the community were vented in 656 in a power struggle, in the course of which Caliph Uthmân was murdered by rebels at his residence in Medina. The opposition installed Alî as caliph; the proclamation took place on June 17, 656 in the mosque of Medina—on the site of the former residence of the Prophet.

According to Shi'i doctrine, with this act the sole legitimate successor to the Prophet finally took power. The Shi'ites do not acknowledge the first three caliphs. They consider Abû Bakr, Umar, and Uthmân as usurpers of the caliphate; for the Shi'ites, ever since Muhammad's death, Alî was the legitimate caliph and imam. "The Imamate of the Commander of the faithful, peace be on him, was for thirty years after the Prophet, may God bless him and his family. For twenty-four years and six months of these he was prevented from administering the laws (of the office) (and had to) exercise precautionary dissimulation *(taqiyya)* and withdrawal.[2] The Shi'ites often explain Alî's restraint with God's plan of salvation: the usurpation by the first three caliphs was preordained to test the community and separate the true believers from the hypocrites *(munâfiqûn)*.

Alî's short caliphate (656-661) was filled with bloody struggle, in which the unity of the Islamic umma was broken forever, a mere two decades after the death of the Prophet. Alî was not generally recognized. He was forced to leave Medina and retreat to Iraq, where he settled in the city of Kufa *(al-Kûfa)* on the Euphrates, an Arabic garrison town from the time of the conquest. His adversary was the governor of Syria, Mu'âwiya of the Umayad clan. Mu'âwiya, a relative of the murdered caliph Uthmân, spoke out in support of the blood feud against Alî. Aside from the mentioned tensions in the umma, regional differences also surfaced in this conflict: Syrian Arabs opposed Iraqi Arabs, Damascus versus Kufa. The two armies faced each other for weeks in the summer of 657 on the battlefields of Siffîn, on the upper Euphrates (in the region of the present Assad Dam in Syria). Despite numerous battles, none was decisive, and in the end an arbitration was arranged, which presumably convened in early 659 in Adhruh (in present-day Jordan between Petra and Ma'ân). The decision of the two arbitrators is not clear, as the reports passed down are contradictory. In any case, Mu'âwiya of Syria interpreted the judgment in his own favor and had tribute paid to himself as caliph in the summer of 660 in Jerusalem. He was widely recognized, thus sealing the division of the umma.

Only half a year later, in late January 661, Alî was slain at the entrance to a mosque in Kufa by the avenger Ibn Muljam; he died from his injuries two days later, at the age of 62 or 63. With that, the first Shi'i imam had fallen, the first in a long line of martyrs of the Shi'a.

The Arabic word *shî'a* means "party." *Shî'at Alî* is "Alî's Party," denoting Alî's followers in his conflict with Mu'âwiya and the Syrians. This "Party" continued to exist even after Alî was murdered. His residence in Kufa on the Euphrates became the stronghold of the "partisans." This is where his comrades-in-arms from Siffîn lived and where they hoped that one of Alî's sons would come into his father's inheritance, once again turning the tides. The Iraqis felt deep hostility toward the governor sent from Damascus, the new capital of the caliphate.

The resistance of the Shi'a at this time had not yet assumed a specifically religious character. It was merely a party in the struggle for power, initially in the generation of the former companions of the Prophet (Alî and Mu'âwiya) and then in the generation of their sons. Since the Shi'ites consider Alî to be the only rightful successor to the Prophet, he alone was assumed to have the right to the military title of the caliph, "Commander of the Faithful" *(amîr al-mu'minîn)*. This is how most Shi'ites refer to Alî, without explicitly mentioning his name. As a symbol of his power of command, he inherited the sword of the Prophet, *Dhû l-Fiqâr,* which is present on all pictorial representations of him.[3] Alî's image was immediately idealized by his supporters and shrouded in legend. He became the prototype of the youthful hero, as in the popular story of how he is said to have displayed superhuman strength during the siege of the oasis town of Khaybar by lifting the city gate from its hinges, using it as a shield, and then flinging it into a ditch. Alî is regarded as the masterful ruler of the Arabic language. Speeches and letters attributed to him, though collected much later (and whose authenticity is disputed), are still considered classic examples of Arabic prose. Alî's grave is also surrounded by wonders: At his own bidding, Alî is said to have been carried into the desert on a bier by his sons, al-Hasan and al-Husayn, as well as other close friends. According to legend, they carried him out to a white rock that radiated light. While digging his grave, a shield was found bearing the inscription: "This is one of the things which Noah has stored for Alî ibn Abî Tâlib."[4] Today, the shrine of Najaf *(an-Najaf)* is located at the site of Alî's grave.

2. The Abdication of al-Hasan (661)

Alî left behind two sons from his marriage to the Prophet's daughter, Fâtima. The elder, al-Hasan, was 36 or 37 years old at the time of his father's death. If he had raised a claim to the caliphate, he could have reckoned with the support of the Kufan party followers of his father, i.e., the Shi'a. He was in fact proclaimed caliph, but when Mu'âwiya moved into Iraq at the head of the Syrian army, al-Hasan appeared indecisive and hesitant.

Negotiations followed in al-Madâ'in on the Tigris—the ancient Ctesiphon—and in the end al-Hasan renounced his claim to the caliphate. A substantial sum of money and the cession of tax revenues of an entire Iranian province compensated for the abdication by the grandson of the Prophet.

Caliph Mu'âwiya occupied the Iraqi metropolis of Kufa; al-Hasan entered the mosque there and publicly announced his abdication, much to the disappointment of Alî's Party.

Al-Hasan returned to Medina, where he lived until his death as a wealthy grand seigneur, never again getting involved in political conflict. His only renown mentioned in historical sources were his numerous marriages and large number of offspring. Not even the year of his death is known conclusively. He must have died between 670 and 680 and is buried in the Al-Baqî' cemetery in Medina.

The Shi'ites consider al-Hasan the rightful successor to his father, Alî, and the second imam, his imamate continuing up until his death. As regards his acquiescence to Mu'âwiya, it is explained in Shi'i sources that in view of the military superiority of the Syrians, the imam wanted to avoid unnecessary fighting and bloodshed among Muslims. He is said to have bowed to the power without renouncing his rights. As all other imams, al-Hasan is viewed by the Shi'ites as a martyr: Mu'âwiya supposedly arranged that al-Hasan be poisoned by one of his wives.

3. The Tragedy of Karbalâ (680)

Caliph Mu'âwiya died in the spring of 680 after designating his son, Yazîd, to be his successor. Yazîd was the first man to become caliph who had not known the Prophet Muhammad personally. At the same time, his succession to the throne established the dynastic principle. The dynasty of the Umayyad clan ruled in Damascus until the year 750.

The transfer of the throne in Damascus represented a signal

for the Iraqi members of Alî's Party to once again attempt to seize power. Alî's second son by Fâtima, al-Husayn, who lived in Medina, was already about 54 years old when Mu'âwiya died. Messengers from Kufa sought him out and pressured him to go to Iraq to head the "Party" in overthrowing the Syrian regime. Al-Husayn sent his cousin Muslim to Kufa to investigate the situation. Muslim reported that conditions were favorable; thousands of supporters were prepared to join the uprising. Although he had been forewarned of danger, al-Husayn then secretly left Mecca, where he had gone on a pilgrimage, in September 680. He made his way to Iraq along the pilgrim route across the desert of central Arabia, accompanied by his family and a small group of supporters—relatives and friends— not more than fifty in all.

Al-Husayn's actions were known in Iraq. The Iraqi governor, Ubaydallâh ibn Ziyâd, had the desert route monitored by patrols. The leading rebels in Kufa, including al-Husayn's cousin Muslim, were executed. Al-Husayn did not get word of this until he was already approaching the Euphrates. Never-theless, he continued on his way. A patrol sent by the governor blocked al-Husayn's way to Kufa, forcing his small group to the north. Of the thousands of "partisans" that supposedly existed in Kufa, not a single one came to the aid of the grandson of the Prophet.

On the second day of the month of Muharram (2 October 680), al-Husayn's troups camped at Karbalâ, 70 kilometers north of Kufa and 20 kilometers west of the Euphrates. Larger contingents of the governor's troops arrived the next day—sup-posedly 4000 men. Under the command of Ibn Sa'd, they blocked access to the river, forcing al-Husayn's troops to do without water for three days. Further negotiations failed, since al-Husayn refused to pay tribute to the caliph Yazîd. On the ninth of Muharram, the Kufan troops approached al-Husayn's camp and early the following morning (10 Muharram/10 October 680), hand-to-hand combat and skirmishes ensued. By afternoon, the camp had been stormed. Al-Husayn and almost

Fig. 1: Imam al-Husayn in battle with his enemies

Fig. 2: Al-Husayn's older son Alî al-Akbar dies in the arms
of his father

Fig. 3: Young Abdullâh flees from his murderer into the
arms of his uncle al-Husayn.

Fig. 4: Al-Husayn gazes at the bodies of his relatives;
at the top, the beheaded infant Alî al-Asghar;
at the bottom, the armless al-Abbâs.

Fig. 5: Shemir chops off al-Husayn's head; in the upper right,
the captured fourth imam Alî Zayn al-Âbidîn.

all the men in his convoy—according to Shi'i tradition, 32 horsemen and 40 foot soldiers—had been killed, including al-Husayn's half-brother al-Abbâs, his son Alî the elder (Alî al-Akbar), and his younger nephew al-Qâsim, a son of al-Hasan.

The casualties were buried at the site of the massacre, where, today, the shrines of Karbalâ are located. Al-Husayn's head was brought to Kufa, where the governor Ubaydallâh ibn Ziyâd is said to have knocked out several teeth with his staff. The captured women, among them al-Husayn's sister Zaynab, and al-Husayn's sole surviving son, Alî the younger (the fourth imam), were sent first to Kufa and then Damascus. There, according to the historical sources, the caliph treated them honorably and released them to go to Medina.

There are reports that Al-Husayn's head was buried in Damascus. His grave is honored to this day in a chamber in the courtyard of the Umayyad mosque of Damascus. According to another tradition, the head was buried in Ascalon in Palestine and was later brought to Cairo to save it from the Crusaders. Al-Husayn's martyr shrine (al-mashhad al-Husaynî) is located in Cairo next to the Azhar mosque.

The earliest reports of the events of Karbalâ were written down by Abû Mikhnaf (died 774) of Kufa, a Shi'ite who was the first to transcribe the stories that had been circulating by oral tradition. His collection has been used by both Sunni and Shi'i historians.[5]

This early historical tradition was quite rational despite the fact that it already carried a Shi'i bias. It did not become obscured by legend until the thirteenth century, when all the moving, horrifying and bloody episodes emerged that continue today to be the preferred topics of the Shi'i passion play and the subject matter of traditional works of art. Alî the younger (Alî al-Asghar), whose existence has not been verified historically, is often portrayed as an infant whose throat is pierced by an arrow. While attempting to fetch water from the Euphrates for his parched companions, al-Husayn's half-brother al-Abbâs gets his right and then his left arm cut off. And especially the imam's nephew, al-Hasan's son al-Qâsim, who is depicted in the earliest representations as a handsome young boy, became a hero of a romantic tragedy in later traditions: Engaged to marry a daughter of his uncle al-Husayn, the young groom falls on his wedding day. The wedding tent that already stands takes up his bier. Even the scene of the surviving women and the sole surviving son before the caliph Yazîd in Damascus and their humiliation by the tyrants was dramatically embellished during this time.

The events of the year 680 are seen by historians as part of the political power struggles within the second generation (al-Husayn ibn Alî versus Yazîd ibn Mu'âwiya). In this view, Karbalâ means nothing more than the elimination of a poorly equipped and indecisive pretender. Religious historians would argue that it was al-Husayn's demise that was actually responsible for the emergence of the Shi'a as a religious phenomenon. There was no religious aspect to Shi'ism prior to 680. The death of the third imam and his followers marked the "big bang" that created the rapidly expanding cosmos of Shi'ism and brought it into motion. For Shi'ites, Karbalâ represents the central point in their belief, the climax of a divine plan of salvation, the promises of which are offered to all who take the side of the martyred imam.

4. The Origins of Shi'i Religious Tradition: The Campaign of the "Penitents" (684)

"Alî's Party" did not take on religious characteristics until *after* the catastrophe of Karbalâ, that is, not until it failed politically. Although there were repeated attempts at a putsch by descendants of both al-Hasan and al-Husayn, none proved successful. In the aftermath of such failure, a large segment of the Shi'ites, including the imams, withdrew from the political state and the Shi'a became an oppositional sect.

The center and starting point of both political and religious Shi'ism was the Iraqi metropolis of Kufa on the Euphrates, originally settled by Arabs. The Shi'a thus emerged in Iraq in a purely Arabic environment. This must be emphasized since it is claimed again and again that Shi'ism is an Iranian phenomenon totally foreign to the Arab mentality. It very well may be that in later centuries, especially after the Shi'ization of Iran in the sixteenth century, a whole series of ancient Iranian traditions found their way into the Shi'i faith. We will take up this question later on when presenting the Âshûrâ rites. In its origins, however, the Shi'a is just as Arabic as Islam itself.

Shi'ism actually began sometime between the dramatic events of Karbalâ (680) and the death march of the Kufan "penitents" in the year 684. We have seen that although the Kufan members of "Alî's Pary" encouraged Alî's son, al-Husayn, to seize power and invited him to Iraq to do so, in the end—certainly under pressure of the Umayyad governor of Kufa—they shamefully did not come to al-Husayn's aid. Not a hand was raised when the imam was threatened in Karbalâ. The tragedy experienced by the grandson of the Prophet gave rise to a severe crisis of conscience among the Kufan "partisans." A group formed that has been remembered as "the penitents" (at-tawwâbûn), comprising what could be called the core of the Shi'a.

The leader of the penitents was a man named Sulaymân ibn Surad, a distinguished Arab and long-standing "partisan," who had fought at Alî's side as far back as the battle of Siffîn. Like most who shared his views, Sulaymân was already in his sixties when Imam al-Husayn was defeated at Karbalâ. His house in Kufa was a regular meeting place for leading "party" personalities, who met to indulge in endless self-reproach. They regretted their failing and sought to relieve their consciences through repentance.

The earliest available source on these events—and thus the earliest document for the emergence of Shi'ism itself—is once again a work by the Kufan Shi'ite Abû Mikhnaf (died 774). He collected contemporary reports of survivors, mostly indirectly, though primarily through only a single link. Abû Mikhnaf's presentation of the campaign of the penitents is heroically distorted and stylized in a Shi'i sense but it nonetheless authentically reflects the views and atmosphere of the Shi'ites in Kufa in the decades of the birth of Shi'ism. Most surprising about this old text—almost totally neglected up to now—is the fact that it already demonstrated all the essential elements that characterize the Shi'i religion today.[6]

The self-accusations of the "partisans" who gathered in the house of Sulaymân ibn Surad peaked in acknowledgement of their own shame and their desire to atone for this through death. Verses of the Quran (sura 2:54) were cited that speak of the Israelites who prayed to the golden calf. God spoke to them through Moses, saying: "Thou hath sinned against thyself! Thou shalt now turn with repentance to thy Creator and kill one another!" In a speech, Sulaymân ibn Surad swore to the image of the Israelites, who presented their necks to the sword in repentance, patiently suffering expiatory death. He called to his companions: "And how about you? If you were now called upon to do the same?"

What followed was a discussion of the possibility of a collective expiatory suicide, but this idea was rejected. One of the speakers was quoted as saying: "By God, if I knew that my suicide would free me of my sin and reconcile me with my Lord, then I would kill myself!"

But—he continued—what was permitted of the Israelites back then was—regrettably—denied the Muslims. The Quran forbids suicide just as it forbids the killing of other Muslims (sura 4:29). But one alternative remained: expiatory death on the battlefield. Collective suicide was thus replaced with collective self-sacrifice carried out by the enemy.

The expressions "sin" (dhanb or khata'), "repentance" or "atonement" (tauba), and "punishment" (uqûba), all of which appear in the text, are constitutive elements of Shi'a Islam. They make up the actual core of Shi'i piety. Reference is often made to the similarities between some aspects of the Shi'i faith and Christian ideas—even by Shi'ites themselves. This will be brought up several times in the following. The differences, however, should not be overlooked. The similarities denote, at most, parallels and not conformity. Shi'i "sin" is not an "original" sin, an existential sinfulness that humanity is plagued with from time immemorial, from which it must be redeemed. Instead, it is a historical failure of the entire "party" in a concrete situation. Even future generations are called upon to wash away this blemish from ancient times with one's own blood. Later Shi'ites have the duty to wipe out the guilt of earlier Shi'ites, as well as their own, of course. Even today, Shi'ites answer as follows when asked why they flagellate themselves or wound themselves with swords in the rituals to commemorate Karbalâ: "to show that if we been there at Karbala we would have stood with him [i.e., the imam] and shed our blood and died with him."[7] This is the origin of the Âshûrâ rituals that will be discussed in the second part of this book. They are not mourning rituals, as is often believed, but a ritual of repentance. These actions are an effort to resolve part of the virtually infinite guilt that has accumulated, in hopes that a merciful God will then release the Shi'ites from the remaining punishment that is actually due.

Sulaymân ibn Surad circulated a letter among the "partisans" in Iraq, inviting them to a joint death march. The date—November 684—and meeting place north of Kufa were set and the "penitents" met there—far fewer, however, than originally consented to take part. They moved northward along the River Euphrates toward Syria. They reposed at the field of Karbalâ to spend one night with blackened faces lamenting and crying over the guilt they felt toward the imam and then they moved on. In early January 685 they were stopped near Ayn al-Warda in northern Mesopotamia by Syrian troops and beaten, as expected and hoped for. There were only a few survivors, who, in view of the casualties on the battlefield, were filled with shame that they had survived. Supposedly, one of them said to one of the fallen, "God will have mercy on you, for *you* have spoken the truth and have suffered; but we have lied and have escaped." In other words, you have fulfilled your vow of death, whereas we have shamefully survived. (After the death of Âyatollâh Khomeinî, there were pictures on television of Iranian prisoners of war returning from Iraq who kneeled at his grave, crying and begging for forgiveness that they had not died in battle. It was a sight foreign to Western eyes, but a familiar, centuries-old ritual gesture for Shi'ites, the only difference being that it was made not to the Imam al-Husayn, but the revolutionary leader.)

The Kufan penitents' movement marked the true beginning of Shi'i Islam. It expressed all the essential elements and concepts of Shi'i piety. The willingness for self-sacrifice is the most outstanding feature, and it has remained unchanged to the present day (it was also politically instrumentalized during the revolution of 1978-79 and during the war against Iraq).

A religious community or sect that sets the collective death of its members as its goal cannot be very long-lived, as has been confirmed by contemporary examples in the United States. Shi'ism, on the other hand, has existed for more than 1300 years. The self-sacrifice that the "penitents" in 684-85 actually committed has been ritualized in the Âshûrâ customs. A ritual is by definition something that is repeated over and over at regular intervals. This presupposes that those practicing the ritual will survive the self-sacrifice. The ritual is normally a substitute action: the ritual action—the shedding of one's own blood by flagellation or beating one's brow with a sword—is a surrogate for that which is actually implied—expiatory death—and at the same time assures the actor of its outcome, namely, exoneration from historical guilt. Of course, real expiatory death as substituted by the ritual can also be demanded. Shi'ites are then asked to demonstrate the seriousness of their willingness to perform self-sacrifice. The revolution in Iran showed us the dramatic consequences of that again and again.

5. Withdrawal from Politics:
The Sixth Imam, Ja'far as-Sâdiq (702-765)

Later in 685, the same year as the sacrifice of the "penitents," the Shi'ites of Kufa rose up against the governor of the caliph and took over the city. A terrible punishment was imposed upon those responsible for the massacre of Karbalâ. Shi'i rule over the city of Kufa and portions of southern Iraq lasted only a year and a half, however, and then collapsed. Instead of al-Husayn's surviving son Alî, the rebels declared a half-brother of al-Hasan and al-Husayn, a man named Muhammad, to be the imam. Muhammad was indeed a son of Alî, but Fâtima was not his mother; in other words, he was not a grandson of the Prophet (see genealogical tree on page 23). This shows that Shi'ism was not yet limited to a particular line of imams. All of Alî's sons were regarded as equal whether or not they were born of Fâtima.

The man the Shi'ites consider the fourth imam was al-Husayn's son Alî, the only surviving relative from the massacre of Karbalâ, during which he lay sick in a tent and was therefore spared. Along with the captured women, he was first brought to the court of the caliph in Damascus and then released to Medina. According to Shi'i tradition, he was given the epithet *Zayn al-Âbidîn,* "the adornment of God's servants." He never entered the political stage and little is known of him and his life. Not even the year he died is known conclusively, though he died some time around 713 in Medina. Just as mysterious was the fifth Imam, Muhammad *al-Bâqir,*[8] who died in 733 in Medina, also without ever having expressed any political ambitions.

Muhammad's half-brother, Zayd, on the other hand, ventured yet another revolt in 739-40 in Kufa, but he was killed in battle against the troops of Caliph Hishâm. His younger son Yahyâ also died in battle in 743 in eastern Iran. In northern Yemen, a Shi'i denomination that follows Zayd is still in existence. The Zaydis do not recognize any firm line of imams, acknowledging instead that any of Muhammad's descendants who fight with the sword for the right of succession can become the imam.

The Shi'a once again assumed more definitive contours through the sixth imam Ja'far. He was presumably born in 702 in Medina and spent his life there as a wealthy landowner. He did not get involved in political activities and died in Medina in 765. The overthrow of the caliphate occurred during his lifetime in the Abbasid Revolution of 749-50. The dynasty of the Umayyads of Damascus was toppled and the Abbasid family took over. The Abbasids were descendants of al-Abbâs, an uncle of the Prophet Muhammad, that is, a member of the Hâshim clan and thus closely related to the imams.

The Iraqi Shi'ites not only welcomed the putsch, they actually helped pave the way for it in hopes of finally coming to power. At the height of the chaos of the revolution, Kufan "partisans" are said to have offered Imam Ja'far as-Sâdiq the caliphate via letter, but he supposedly declined. His reasons, assuming the truth of the reports, are not known. In any case, the Shi'ites went away empty-handed and were soon pushed aside by the new Abbasid Dynasty; they remained in the opposition.

Ja'far as-Sâdiq kept in close contact with the Shi'ites in Iraq but continued to refrain from any political activity whatsoever, and was thus left in peace by the new rulers. He even traveled to Iraq, probably to pay homage to the Abbasid caliph al-Mansûr (754-775), at which time he is said to have rediscovered the lost grave of the first imam, Alî, near an-Najaf.

In 762—three years before the death of Imam Ja'far—Caliph al-Mansûr established a new capital near the village of Baghdâd on the Tigris. It quickly developed into the main metropolis in Iraq. At the beginning of the ninth century, under Caliph Hârûn ar-Rashîd, it was already the largest city in the contemporary world, measuring about 10 kilometers in diameter. In addition to Kufa, Baghdad became another major center of Shi'ism in Iraq. A large number of Shi'ites settled at the outskirts of the capital, especially in the southern suburb of al-Karkh, though they represented only a minority of the total population.

The Twelve Imams

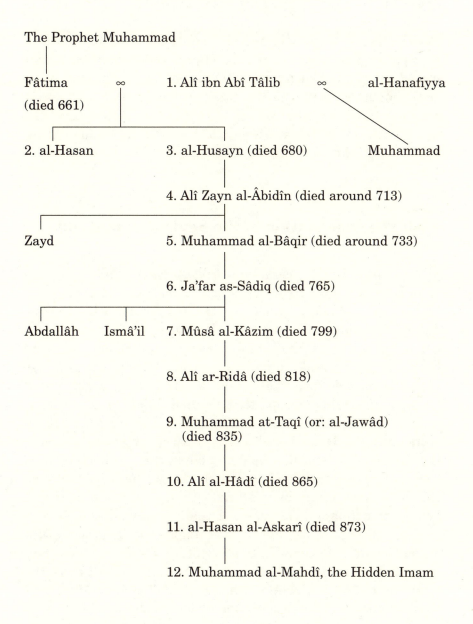

The Prophet Muhammad

Fâtima   ∞   1. Alî ibn Abî Tâlib   ∞   al-Hanafiyya
(died 661)

2. al-Hasan   3. al-Husayn (died 680)   Muhammad

4. Alî Zayn al-Âbidîn (died around 713)

Zayd   5. Muhammad al-Bâqir (died around 733)

6. Ja'far as-Sâdiq (died 765)

Abdallâh   Ismâ'il   7. Mûsâ al-Kâzim (died 799)

8. Alî ar-Ridâ (died 818)

9. Muhammad at-Taqî (or: al-Jawâd)
   (died 835)

10. Alî al-Hâdî (died 865)

11. al-Hasan al-Askarî (died 873)

12. Muhammad al-Mahdî, the Hidden Imam

The sixth imam, Ja'far as-Sâdiq, is regarded to be the founder of Shi'i law. As a private scholar in Medina, the imam collected and commented on traditions of the Prophet Muhammad.
The Shi'ites thus consider him the most significant authority in
all legal and religious questions. Handbooks on Shi'i law that
were later published included thousands of comments by the
sixth imam. This is why the Shi'ites named their faith after
him, the "ja'faritic legal school." According to article 12 of the
constitution of the Islamic Republic, the official religion of Iran
is Islam and the "ja'faritic legal school."

6. The Deportation of the Seventh Imam (796)

The death of Ja'far as-Sâdiq in 765 threw the Shi'i community in Iraq into a severe crisis, since the successor to the imam
had not yet been determined. Ja'far's son Ismâ'îl, who was evidently designated as successor, had already died ten years
before his father, and Ja'far's firstborn, Abdallâh, only survived
his father by several months, leaving no heirs of his own (see
genealogical tree, page 23). There are reports of a half dozen
larger and smaller groups that became followers of different
imams, leading to the first major split in Shi'ism. Of all these
sects, only the Ismailis still exist today. They are followers of
the imamate of Ismâ'îl, who died young, and his descendants.
The current leader of the Ismailis, the Agha Khan, is considered
the forty-ninth imam in this line. Other members of this sect
believe that Imam Ja'far never actually died and still lives in
hiding, waiting one day to return triumphantly. This is our first
encounter with the belief in the "occultation" (ghayba) of a "hidden" imam. This idea initially received little support, since the
sixth imam had left behind other sons. Ja'far's son Mûsâ was
consequently widely recognized as the seventh imam. But in its
formative phase, Shi'ism fluctuated several times between the
model of an incarnate, present imam and that of an absent,

"hidden" imam, before the "occultation" model finally found widespread acceptance.

The seventh iman, called *al-Kâzim* (the reserved or self-controlled one) by the Shi'ites, initially lived, as did all his predecessors, in Medina. In 795-96, however, when Caliph Hârûn ar-Rashîd came to Mecca and Medina on a pilgrimage, he brought the imam with him upon returning to Iraq, holding him under house arrest, first in Basra and later in Baghdad. By this time the followers of the imam were apparently so large in number that the caliph was frightened of them and assured the imam's personal safety. From this time forward, all imams were held in Iraq under the guardianship of the caliphs of Baghdad, even if as descendants of the Prophet they were not harmed. According to Shi'i tradition, this Babylonian captivity of the imams is described as a long chain of martyrdoms. According to the Shi'i faith, all imams without exception were eliminated in a violent manner by the caliphs, usually through poison (though this is not confirmed). The death of the seventh imam, Mûsâ, in 799 provided the first opportunity to spread such rumors. Mûsâ al-Kâzim was buried at the cemetery of the Arabic aristocracy north of Baghdad. Above his grave, the Shi'i shrine with two golden domes can be seen today in al-Kâzimiyya, an outlying district named after him. His grandson, the ninth imam, is buried next to him. The suburban district used to be called *al-Kâzimayn,* "the two Kâzims," after the graves of the two imams.

7. The Eighth Imam Alî ar-Ridâ as Heir Apparent (816)

The eighth imam, Alî *ar-Ridâ* (the agreeable one, Pers. *Rezâ),* lived in Medina after his father was deported, but was then also brought eastward in 816 by al-Ma'mûn, Hârûn ar-Rashîd's son and successor. He traveled to the caliph's residence at that time

in Merv (now Mary in Turkmenistan), at the farthest end of the
empire. Once there, the approximately fifty-year-old imam was
surprisingly given one of the caliph's daughters' hand in marriage and more than that: Not only did the caliph make him a
son-in-law, but he also proclaimed Alî ar-Ridâ to be his successor. There has been much speculation about this spectacular
step by Caliph al-Ma'mûn. The explanation lies in the contemporary political state of affairs, which will not be considered further here, since it remained an isolated incident. As the caliph
was marching westward, namely, to subjugate the princes who
were revolting in Baghdad after having been excluded from the
succession, Imam Alî ar-Ridâ died in 818 in the city of Tûs in
eastern Iran and was buried nearby. The present-day city of
Mashhad grew up around his grave, the "shrine of the martyr"
(Arabic *al-mashhad)*. It is the only grave of an imam that is
located within Iran. Even today, the grave is a site of pilgrimage, where Shi'ites loudly curse the caliphs al-Ma'mûn and his
father, Hârûn ar-Rashîd, the torturers of the seventh and
eighth imams.

8. The Shrine of Qom

There is another shrine in Iran aside from the one in Mashhad that played an outstanding role as a pilgrimage site for
devout Iranian Shi'ites through the ages: it is in Qom. In the
twentieth century it even became the intellectual and, for a
time being, political center of the Shi'a.

This ancient Iranian city, approximately 140 kilometers
southwest of present-day Tehran on a salt-water river at the
edge of the desert, was most likely destroyed during the Arabic-
Islamic conquest, but was resettled in 712 by Arab colonists
who had had to leave Kufa for reasons of their Shi'i beliefs. The
Islamic city of Qom was thus a Shi'i city from the outset, an off-
shoot of Kufa, retaining its Arabic character until into the tenth

century. When Fâtima *al-Ma'sûma* (the infallible one), sister of the eighth imam, traveled to eastern Iran in 817 to visit her brother, who had been proclaimed heir apparent, she fell ill in the city of Sâveh, west of Qom. In order to live her final days among Shi'ites, she arranged to be brought to Qom, where she died and was buried. The golden dome on her tomb dominates the townscape of Qom to this day. Not only did Qom become a pilgrimage site for Shi'ites, but a large number of well-known Shi'i scholars and authors in the ninth and tenth centuries came from there.

9. The Imams in Sâmarrâ (836-873)

The ninth imam, Muhammad al-Jawâd (the liberal one), also called at-Taqî (the God-fearer), was already married to a daughter of Caliph al-Ma'mûn as a child, in order to create close ties to the ruling dynasty. After a time, he was allowed to return to Medina from Baghdad with his family. In 835, however, Caliph al-Mu'tasim, brother and successor to al-Ma'mûn, once again called for the then twenty-four-year-old imam, who returned to Baghdad and died in the same year. He was buried next to his grandfather Mûsâ al-Kâzim in the elite cemetery north of the capital; the double grave of "the two Kâzims" *(al-Kâzimayn)* still stands out today with its two adjacent golden domes.

A year later Caliph al-Mu'tasim left Baghdad and settled with his Turkish guards in the new residence he founded in Sâmarrâ, about 100 kilometers northwest of Baghdad, on the Tigris. For more than half a century (836-892), Sâmarrâ was the caliphate capital, and the imams were required to follow the caliphs there. In 848 Caliph al-Mutawakkil had the tenth imam, Alî al-Hâdî (the guide to what is right), brought to Sâmarrâ, where he died in 868 at about forty years of age; he was buried in his home. There were certainly political reasons for the renewed deportation of an imam. The Shi'a had become

so strong over time that it posed a serious threat. The fact that
a caliphal order was issued in 850 to destroy the pilgrimage
shrine of the Shi'ites above al-Husayn's grave in Karbalâ clearly shows the extent to which the Shi'ites were feared by the
caliphs.

The eleventh iman, al-Hasan, was given the epithet
al-Askarî, since he had been forced to live in the caliph's army
camp *(askar)* in Sâmarrâ. When he died on December 25, 873 or
January 1, 874, at the age of twenty-eight, he was interred
beside his father on the grounds of his own residence. The gold-
en-domed shrine of "the two Askarîs" *(al-Askariyyayn)*, i.e. the
tenth and eleventh imams, is now located at this site.

10. The Occultation of the Twelfth Imam (873)

According to common—especially Sunni—tradition, when the
eleventh imam died at such a young age, he left no male heir.
The oldest Shi'i sources also confirm that the apparent end to
the main line of imams threw the Shi'i communities in Iraq and
Qom into a serious crisis. There was much difference of opinion
among "Party" members as to who should lead the umma as the
imam. As a result the Shi'a splintered into more than a dozen
different groups and sects. This phase of their history is referred to in Shi'i tradition as the period of "confusion" *(hayra)*.

One of these groups claimed from the very beginning that the
eleventh imam did not die without having produced a child;
rather, he is said to have had a son named Muhammad who was
born in 869. According to these sources, before he reached the
age at which he was transferred from the realm of the women
to that of the men, thus appearing in public, he was hidden by
his father to protect him from the caliph. Only the closest family members and a few trusted friends—according to Shi'i tradition—had ever glimpsed this twelfth imam before he was hidden. Even when the eleventh imam died, his rightful successor

did not step forward. He has remained hidden somewhere on the earth since then, but he will supposedly reappear one day and take his position at the head of the "Party," asserting the legitimate rights of his family line.

The idea of a concealed or occult imam was nothing new. Even after the deaths of Alî's third son Muhammad, the sixth imam Ja'far as-Sâdiq, and the seventh imam Mûsâ al-Kâzim, some people believed for a time that they had not died, but were merely hidden, waiting to return a short time later. Some Shi'ites had similar hopes with respect to the twelfth imam, even though no one had ever seen him. It took almost two hundred years until the belief in the existence of the Hidden Imam became widely accepted throughout the Shi'i community, at which time the other circles and sects that had emerged during the period of "confusion" disappeared. The Imâmiyya Shi'ites thus became the "Twelvers" (Ithnâ'ashariyya), as they refer to themselves to distinguish themselves from other Shi'i groups. Belief in the existence of the hidden twelfth imam and his future return became the most important distinguishing feature.

It is important to remember that the twelfth imam is imagined as living in hiding somewhere on the earth. Initially he was believed to be living incognito on Byzantine territory to remain completely out of the clutches of the caliph. For four generations it was also believed that the Hidden Imam was connected to his "orphaned" community through a messenger (safîr), giving his commands via letter. Such letters actually circulated throughout the communities and are still passed down today. The Shi'ites refer to this period (874-941) as the "lesser occultation" (al-ghayba as-sughrâ). After that, the Hidden Imam decided to break off all contact and retreat totally from humanity. In his last letter, he is said to have announced his intention, branding as a liar anyone claiming in the future to have had contact with him. The year 941 thus marked the beginning of the period of the "greater occultation" (al-ghayba al-kubrâ), which continues to the present day. Shi'i communities were thus totally lacking spiritual leadership, an umma without a present imam. This was a very precarious situation, since it raised the question as to who was capable and authorized to guide the community during the absence of the twelfth imam. The history of the Shi'ites can be described as continual wrestling for an answer to this question. The most recent attempt up to now to find an answer was the contemporary revolution in Iran.

11. The Fourteen Infallible Ones

The Prophet Muhammad, his daughter Fâtima, and the twelve imams are referred to by the Shi'ites as "the fourteen infallible ones" (Pers. *chahâr-dah ma'sûm).* The word *ma'sûm,* borrowed from the Arabic, actually means protected or immune, since the Fourteen are considered immune to error and sin. Comments or written announcements they made enjoy unrestricted authority; every member of the faith can count on them absolutely.

The Sunnis have granted only the passed-down comments of Muhammad such absolute authority, and they view this collection alone as the binding "practice" *(sunna)* for all Muslims. The Shi'ites, on the other hand, have also collected the statements of the Prophet that have been confirmed by eye and ear witnesses, as well as those of Fâtima and the twelve imams. Such collections form the foundation of Sunni and Shi'i law, respectively (this will be discussed in the chapter on Shi'i legal scholars, the mullahs).

It is significant that the Shi'ites accept the quality of infallibility only for the Fourteen. No other person dare claim such authority. This pertains even to the highest âyatollâhs; even they are capable of error, and all their decisions and judgments are therefore of provisional nature and always subject to revision (this procedure will also be discussed in the chapter on the mullahs). The fact that infallibility is limited to these fourteen authorities, of which thirteen are already dead and the fourteenth is hidden, has proved to be especially favorable and practicable for the further development of Shi'ism. The existing authorities are all fallible human beings who have been granted free rein for their own actions, which are all provisional and thus subject to revision.

The imams have yet something else in common: they are also considered martyrs. Not only Alî, who was murdered in Kufa, and al-Husayn, slaughtered in the Karbalâ massacre; not only the imams deported to Iraq and killed in prison, but also those who seem to have died a natural death in Medina—all were eliminated by the respective rulers, according to Shi'i tradition. The entire family of the Prophet is thus called the "House of Sorrow" *(bait al-ahzân)*. The anniversary of the death, of martyrdom, of each of the imams is celebrated by Shi'ites as a day of mourning. Only the twelfth imam is commemorated on his birthday (15th of Sha'bân). There are also traditions according to which even the hidden twelfth imam will suffer martyrdom once he returns, so that he, too, will be given the honorable title of a martyr *(shahîd)*, the highest title granted by the Shi'ites.

Since the imams are infallible and without sin, they did not deserve to be martyred; they suffer even though they are innocent. It is also assumed that they all accepted their fate knowingly and willingly, especially al-Husayn, who is said not to have set off for Iraq to claim the power of the caliphate, but to seek the martyred death that God had forseen for him. Just as Jesus went to Jerusalem to die on the cross, al-Husayn went to Karbalâ to accept the passion that had been meant for him from the beginning of time. Shi'i theologians do not neglect to draw parallels between Jesus and the "prince of martyrs." In some Shi'i texts, al-Husayn experiences a moment of doubt on the day before Karbalâ similar to that of Jesus in the garden of Gethsemane. Another legend tells the story of Jesus and his disciples passing through the plain of Karbalâ. They see a herd of gazelles, crowding together and weeping. According to tradition, Jesus also begins to weep, explaining to his disciples that at this site, the youthful son of the Prophet Muhammad would one day be killed.[9]

Parallels to Christian ideas also come up when the martyrdom of innocent imams is interpreted as surrogate suffering that brings redemption. French Orientalist Henry Corbin spoke in this context of Shi'i "Christology." The differences to Christian beliefs are obvious, however. The Shi'a, as well as Sunni Islamic thought, includes neither the concept of an inherited, original sin, nor one of a constitutional sinfulness of humankind. Hence there is also no concept of redemption, for which there is no corresponding word in Islamic terminology. Guilt always refers to a historical—individual or collective—guilt that must be atoned. The Fourteen Infallible Ones voluntarily assume a portion of that punishment which is actually meant for sinful people—of course, this refers only to the "partisans," the Shi'ites. Their surrogate suffering spares humanity from experiencing God's full judgment. The merit of self-sacrifice authorizes the Fourteen to assume the role of mediator (wasîla) between God and humanity and to speak out in favor (shafâ'a) of their sinful followers—the Shi'ites—at the Last Judgment. Fâtima's role as a mediator at the Last Judgment is especially emphasized.

The idea of the preexistence of the imams developed very early. Although it is always stressed that they are not eternal—as only God is—and they are born into the world as human beings and then die and are resurrected, their souls are said to be the first of God's creations, created before all other beings, in the form of light. They are thus not of dust, but of light. According to the fifth imam, Imam Alî himself is to have said: "God . . . is One . . . unique in His unity. He uttered a word which became a light. From that light He created Muhammad and created me and my progeny. Then God uttered another word which became a spirit, which He made to dwell in that light and the light He made to dwell in our bodies. Thus we [the imams] are the spirit of God and His words."[10] Shi'i theologians had constantly to guard against the temptation to idolize the imams. Some marginal Shi'i groups, condemned by orthodox theologians as "exaggerators" *(ghulât),* succumbed to this temptation. Their tradition, according to which especially Alî is afforded divine status and Muhammad is seen as his prophet, lives on today in the Syrian sect of the Alawîs, or Nusayrîs.

The great status that even orthodox Twelver Shi'ites attach to the imams can be appreciated through the notion that the existence of an imam is absolutely imperative for the continuation of the world. If there were no imam, according to Shi'i belief, the cosmos would immediately cease to exist. This idea is, on the other hand, often used as evidence of the existence of the Hidden Imam. The fact that the world continues to exist is considered proof that there must be a Hidden Imam.

The Fourteen play an important role in popular religious customs. Making visits *(ziyâra)* to their graves and crying over their fated suffering are considered very commendable acts. Through religious endowments *(waqf)* established by private persons or rulers, their shrines in an-Najaf, Karbalâ, al-Kâzimayn near Baghdad, Mashhad, and Sâmarrâ have grown in the course of centuries into huge economic enterprises that own land throughout the world. Ever since Shi'i monarchs have been ruling in Iran (1501), golden domes have been built on the tombs. The names of the imams, together with their respective epithets, are popular male first names. For example, the first name of the Âyatollâh al-Hakîm, leader of the Shi'ites of southern Iraq who is living in Tehran in exile, is Muhammad Bâqir (after the fifth imam). Even the descendants of the imams, called imâm-zâdes in Iran, enjoy high regard and are honored as local saints after their death. The domed mausoleums of the imâm-zâdes can be seen throughout Iran. Most famous are the shrines of the sister of the eighth imam in Qom and that of Abdal'azîm in Rey, south of Tehran. Their first names, too, are very popular, especially those of the sons killed at Karbalâ and other relatives of al-Husayn (the current foreign minister of Iran, Velâyatî, is named Alî Akbar, after al-Husayn's oldest son).

The living descendants of the first eleven imams, i.e., all natural descendants of the Prophet Muhammad, currently number in the thousands. They are called sherifs (Arabic *sharîf* means noble one) and have the privilege of being allowed to call themselves *sayyid* (sir). They live throughout the entire Islamic world. Only a minority of the descendants of the Prophet are members of the Shi'i faith. Among these descendants are the king of Morocco and the king of Jordan, both Sunnis. Both are Hasanis, descendants of the second imam. Among Shi'ites, the Husaynis of course enjoy particular esteem. As a descendant of the seventh imam, Mûsâ al-Kâzim, Âyatollâh Khomeinî has the family name Mûsawî (the name Khomeinî refers to his birthplace, Khomeyn). The Shi'i sayyids can be recognized by their headware; they are the only Shi'ites allowed to wear a black turban.

12. The Return of the Mahdî

According to Shi'i belief, the missing twelfth imam is living hidden somewhere on the earth. No one knows exactly when he will triumphantly return, though it could happen at any moment. In some Shi'i cities in Iran during the Middle Ages, a saddled horse was held ready at all times so that the imam could mount it upon his reappearance without any delay. In Article 5 of the 1979 constitution of the Islamic Republic of Iran, the naming of the Hidden Imam—as the true head of state—is followed by the pious wish: "May God speed his return!"

It is no coincidence that the twelfth imam is named Muhammad, since it is his task to complete the mission of the Prophet, his forefather with the same name. The twelfth imam's epithet is *al-Mahdî*, the rightly guided one. This name calls forth eschatological associations in every Muslim. The concept of a future savior and renewer of Islam who will be called the Mahdî is not exclusive to the Shi'ites. It is widespread throughout the entire Islamic world, though the expectation of the Mahdî does not play such a central role in Sunni doctrine. Only the Shi'ites have largely standardized the concepts associated with the Mahdî.

Hopes that God will send a "rightly guided" ruler who will end the political and denominational divisions within Islam and reestablish a unified, pure, original Islam emerged in the epoch at the end of the seventh century, when the unity of the Islamic umma was destroyed in bloody power struggles for the succession to the Prophet. At that time, a number of pretenders were proclaimed by their followers to be the Mahdî or they themselves came forth claiming to be the "rightly guided." Thus the concept of the Mahdî is common to all Islamic denominations that emerged during those confusing times. Hopes for the Mahdî did not take on its current particular expression until it was combined in the Shi'i realm with belief in a Hidden Imam. The first such case was following the death of Alî's third son, Muhammad—the half-brother of al-Hasan and al-Husayn (see above, page 21)—in the year 700. His followers believed that he did not die, but rather remained in Mount Radwâ between Mecca and Medina, waiting for the day of his return. This third son of Alî soon lost importance and fell into oblivion, especially in light of the fact that the descendants of al-Husayn provided living, present imams for the Shi'ites. When the eleventh imam died apparently leaving no heirs and the belief in the existence of a hidden twelfth imam gradually gained acceptance, hopes for the coming of the Mahdî were combined with this figure. The twelfth imam, Muhammad, is believed to be the "rightly guided one," who will one day return "to fill the earth with justice, as it is now filled with injustice."

For the Shi'ites, the twelfth imam is the only legitimate ruler of all Muslims, even though he is absent. For this reason, he is also the true head of state according to the current constitution of the Republic of Iran. The state order that was established in Iran through revolution is thus, theoretically speaking, provisional. The return of the Mahdî has been linked since time immemorial with utopian notions of the reestablishment of the Golden Age that for all Muslims is the time of the Prophet Muhammad. This utopia was easily filled with political content during the Iranian revolution: the kingdom of justice that the Mahdî would establish took the place of classless society or other revolutionary goals.

A text from the late tenth century can serve to illustrate how people imagined the return of the Mahdî. It is taken from the *Kitâb al-Irshâd* (Book of Guidance), a collection of traditions about the twelve imams from the pen of Baghdad Shi'ite, Shaykh al-Mufîd.[11] According to the text, terrible omens would announce the coming of the Mahdî:

". . . there will be an eclipse of the sun in the middle of the month of Ramadân; there will be an eclipse of the moon at the end of that month in contrast to ordinary happenings; the land will be swallowed up at al-Baydâ'; it will be swallowed in the east; it will be swallowed up in the west; the sun will stay still from the time of its decline to the middle of the time for the afternoon prayer; it will rise from the west; . . . black standards will advance from Khurâsân; al-Yamânî will come out in revolt; al-Maghribî will appear in Egypt and take possession of it from Syria; the Turk will occupy the region of al-Jazîra; the Byzantines will occupy Ramla; the star will appear in the east giving light just like the moon gives light; then (the new moon) will bend until its two tips almost meet; a colour will appear in the sky and spread to its horizons; a fire will appear for a long time in the east remaining in the air for three or seven days; . . . the Euphrates will flood so that the water comes into the alleys of Kûfa; sixty liars will come forward, all of them claiming prophethood, and twelve will come forward from the family of Abû Tâlib, all of them claiming the Imamate; . . . a black wind will raise it at the beginning of the day and then an earthquake will occur so that much of it will be swallowed up; fear will cover the people of Iraq and Baghdâd; swift death (will occur) there and there will be a loss of property, lives and harvests; locusts will appear at their usual times and at times not usual so that they attack agricultural land and crops and there will be little harvest for what the people planted; two kinds of foreigners will dispute and much blood will be shed in their quarrel; slaves will rebel against obedience to their masters and kill their masters (mawâlî); a group of heretics (ahl al-bida') will be transformed until they become monkeys and pigs; . . . a cry (will come) from the sky (in such a way) that all the people will hear it in their own languages; a face and a chest will appear in the sky before the people in the centre of the sun; the dead will arise from their graves so that they will return to the world and they will recognize one another and visit one another; that will come to an end with twenty-four continuous rainstorms and the land will be revived by them after being dead and it will recognize its blessings; after that every disease will be taken away from those of the Shî'a of the Mahdî, peace be on him, who believe in the truth; at that time they will know of his appearance in Mecca and they will go to him to support him."

The year the Mahdî returns is not known, but the day is known to be the 10th of Muharram, the day al-Husayn was martyred at Karbalâ. He will stand opposite the Ka'ba "and Gabriel, peace be on him, on his right will call for the pledge of allegiance to God. His Shî'a will come to him from the ends of the earth, rolling up in great numbers to pledge allegiance to him. Then God will fill the earth with justice just as it was filled with injustice."

According to a statement made by the fifth imam, it is known what the Mahdî will look like:

"He is a young man of medium stature with a handsome face and beautiful hair. His hair flows on to his shoulders. A light rises on his face. The hair of his beard and head are black."

His kingdom of justice is described as paradise on earth. "In his time, injustice will be removed and the roads will be safe. The earth will produce its benefits and every due will be restored to its proper person. No people of any other religions will remain without being shown Islam and confessing faith in it. . . . At that time men will not find any place to give alms nor be generous because wealth will encompass all the believers."

PART TWO

The Deluge of Weeping Flagellant Procession and Passion Play

1. The Origins of the Âshûrâ Ritual

In 684, four years after the martyrdom of al-Husayn, the "penitents"—committed to performing a collective act of self-sacrifice—passed through the plains of Karbalâ on their march into death. They spent a day and a night at the grave of the imam, wailing and lamenting with blackened faces. This was not so much to honor the death of al-Husayn, as we have seen, as in response to their own feelings of guilt. They prayed to the martyred imam for forgiveness for their failure.

The public display of guilt at the grave of the imam and lamenting over one's own sins are the roots of the large complex of atonement and mourning rituals of the Shi'ites. Most of these rituals take place during the first ten days of the month of al-Muharram, climaxing on the 10th of Muharram or "tenth" *(Âshûrâ)*, the anniversary of al-Husayn's death. They recall the martyrdom of the third imam and enable followers to share in his suffering and atone for a portion of their individual sin as well as the collective, historical guilt of the Shi'a.

At the true core of any religion are the rituals carried out collectively by the believers, and not the ideological web that theologians build around them in retrospect. The community is created not by the profession of belief in dogma but through the process of performing the rituals. For this reason, the rituals of the Shi'ites will be the focus of the following presentation, for this is necessary in grasping the essence of Shi'ism. In contrast to this, the regulatory set of canonical laws of the mullahs and the âyatollâhs, the Shi'i religious scholars, are secondary and will be discussed afterward.

The origin of the Muharram or Âshûrâ rites has been sought in traditions passed down from pre- or non-Islamic sources, such as the ancient oriental lamentation over the slain god of spring Tammûz (Adonis), or the Iranian mythical hero Siyâwush.[1] But it is not even necessary to go that far back in history, especially since the Iranian influence on Shi'ism was minimal during the Middle Ages and did not develop fully until the sixteenth century. It must be kept in mind that Shi'ism was originally a Mesopotamian phenomenon and there, ritual forms such as lamentation as an act of penance and a part of the religious service can definitely be found close—both chronologically and geographically—to the beginnings of the Shi'a. This is true of all larger religious communities in Iraq: Manichaeism as well as Judaism, Christianity, and early Islam. According to Ephrem Syrus of Edessa (died 373), a Christian author, wailing during prayer purifies the body of sin. This type of "wailer" (Arabic *bakkâ'*) was known to Mesopotamian Judaism and Iraqi Islam, for example Rabbi Abraham Qîdônayâ (died 637) and Islamic theologian al-Hasan of Basra (died 728). The Babylonian Talmud even warns that excessive lamentation can lead to blindness.[2]

Collective lamentation at al-Husayn's gravesite in Karbalâ is the oldest documented form of Shi'i ritual. Development and differentiation of the ritual must have taken place very early, even if the individual phases of this development are hardly distinguishable due to the scarcity of original sources. This lack of source material can be explained by the fact that most authors of the Middle Ages were Sunnis who paid little attention to peculiar customs of the Shi'ites, and even among Shi'i authors, most were canonists and jurists more concerned with legal questions than with rituals practiced by the common people.

Nevertheless, isolated reports attest to two forms of penitence and lamentation rituals existing as early as the Middle Ages: (1) an elegy recited by a singer and (2) a procession. Both are still significant today and both contributed to the emergence of the staged scenes of the passion play, the ta'ziyeh.

The elegy (Arabic *marthiya,* pl. *marâthî;* or *nawh;* Persian *nowha* or *mâtam)* tells the story of the tragic events of Karbalâ to a wailing audience. The first step to the dramatization of the events came when silent actors started pantomiming the scenes of the song, which was known to all the participants, who had been hearing the story since childhood. An important dramatic element is also the interplay between singer and audience response. Their chants and set phrases were incorporated into the presentation as a kind of choral refrain in response to the singer's recitation. There are obvious parallels to the ritualistic origins of the Greek tragedy.[3]

The second root of the passion play are the elements of staged scenes, documented even in early processions on the 10th of Muharram. The Shi'ites in Baghdad were allowed to commemorate the events at Karbalâ for the first time publicly in the year 963. The caliph at that time was no longer more than a puppet in the hands of his Iranian commander in chief, Mu'izz ad-Daula, a Bûyid, and his vizier al-Muhallabî. Both were known for their Shi'i leanings and under their protection, Shi'ites were allowed to appear in public to celebrate their festivals, even in Baghdad, which was primarily Sunni. Baghdad chronicler Ibn al-Jawzî wrote the following for the year 963: "On the tenth of Muharram, the markets in Baghdad were closed and all business was suspended. The butchers ceased their slaughtering and the cooks did not cook. Unremittingly people asked for a sip of water. Tents were pitched in the sûqs and draped with felt covers; the women wandered through the market alleys with their hair hanging loose, slapping their faces; lamentations for the martyred al-Husayn could be heard."[4]

This is the earliest known report of the processions on the tenth of Muharram. The description of the ritual corresponds to its present form. The Shi'ites certainly commemorated this event even earlier, but 963 was the first time the festivities were carrried out with official permission. Henceforth there would continually be bloody confrontations with Sunni spectators who felt provoked by the Shi'i ritual, especially the usual invective against prominent companions of the Prophet Muhammad, who were adversaries of the first imam Alî. The short excerpt from the Baghdad chronicle did not only mention the women's lamentation, but also the pitching of tents, meant to represent the camp of al-Husayn and his supporters at Karbalâ, and the procession participants' practice of begging for water, symbolizing the thirst of the martyrs when their access to the Euphrates was barred. These dramatic elements are the very same ones that are part of Âshûrâ processions today.

The Bûyids, a Shi'i condottiere family from northwestern Iran, ruled from 945 to 1055. They did not challenge the Sunni caliphate in Baghdad and were able to offer protection and patronage to the Shi'a in Iraq and northwestern Iran. This is one of the most important epochs in the history of the development of Shi'i ritual, law, and literature. Apparently the number of Shi'ites grew considerably during this period even in the cities of western Iran. In the twelfth century, there were Shi'i communities not only in Qom, but also in Rey (south of present-day Tehran), Varâmîn, Qazvîn, Âveh, Hamadân, Kâshân, and Isfahân, as well as on the southern shore of the Caspian Sea and in the eastern Iranian cities of Sabzavâr, Nîshâpûr, and Tûs. The shrine of the eighth imam Alî ar-Ridâ (Persian *Rezâ*) is in Mashhad, near Tûs. The Shi'a also expanded westward. The residents of the northern Syrian city of Halab (Aleppo) were primarily Shi'ites during that time. At a young age, Mevlânâ Jalâl ad-Dîn Rûmî (died 1273), a mystic, had observed and harshly criticized a Muharram procession before the gates of Aleppo. It did not make sense to him that people mourned a corpse that had long-since decayed. He suggested they lament over their own sins; like many other outside observers, he was not aware that this was precisely what the mourners were doing.

2. European Reports from the Time of the Safavid Dynasty (1501-1722)

In the year 1501 in Tabrîz, Ismâ'îl, the fifteen-year-old spiritual ruler of an Azeri dervish sect, was proclaimed king of kings *(shâhân-shâh)* by his Turkoman supporters. He ruled over all of Iran and Iraq until 1510. Ismâ'îl was the founder of the Safavid dynasty, which ruled until 1722 and spread Shi'ism throughout Iran. Ismâ'îl had already declared the Shi'i faith to be the state religion when he took the throne. The majority of the population was still Sunni, however, and there was no Shi'i infrastructure. Since Shi'i scholars with their own traditional education and knowledge structures had not yet been established in Iran, Ismâ'îl and his successors brought Arab scholars into the country from Iraq and the Persian Gulf region, and from South Lebanon, which had been Shi'i since time immemorial. These scholars then ardently pursued the goal of converting the entire country to the Shi'i faith. Many Iranian mullah families still show signs of their Arabic, often Lebanese, heritage. By the end of the seventeenth century, Iran was a predominantly Shi'i country; a true Shi'i "clergy" had developed.

The earliest extant reports written by western travelers that offer a detailed description of the Muharram rites are from the Safavid period; the oldest of these, *A Relation of Some Yeares Travaile into Afrique, Asia, Indies,* was written by Thomas Herbert, an Englishman, and published in 1634 in London. He reported the following:

"They celebrate the death of *Hussan* eldest sonne of *Hali,* yearely with many Ceremonies, I haue seene them nine seuerall dayes in great multitudes, in the streets all together crying out *Hussan, Hussan,* so long and fiercely, that many could cry no more hauing spent their voices, they ninth day they find them (whom they imagine lost in a Forrest) or one in his place, and then in a huge hurly burly, men, girles and boyes, crying out *Hussan, Hussan* with Drummes, Fifes, and the like, they bring him to the Mosque, and so after some admiration and thansgiuing they put an end to that their *Orgee.*"[5]

The next report is that of a Turkish traveler who came to the court of Shah Safî I in 1640, one year after the definitive peace treaty between the Safavids and the Ottoman sultans, who were Sunnis. He described the impact of the recitation of a marthiya, an elegy to the death of al-Husayn, on the listening crowd:

"When the reader of the book [on the martyrdom of Hosain] reaches the part describing the manner in which the accursed Shemr killed the oppressed Imam Hosain, at that very moment, they bring out to the field . . . mock representations of the bodies of the dead children of the Imam. Upon seeing this spectacle shouts and screams and wailings of 'Alas, Hosain' mount from the people to the heavens and all spectators weep and wail. Hundreds of Hosain's devotees beat and wound their heads, faces and bodies with swords and knives. For the love of Imam Hosain they make their blood flow. The green grassy field becomes bloodied and looks like a field of poppies. Then the mock dead are carried from the field and the reading of the story of Imam Hosain's martyrdom is completed."[6]

I believe this is the earliest report that mentions self-mortification with swords and knives. Carrying in small boys who symbolize the corpses of the murdered sons of al-Husayn is yet another dramatic element leading up to the later passion play; such "tableaux vivants" are still common in processions today.

Shortly before the journeys of this Turkish traveler, Adam Olearius traveled through Tsarist Russia and Iran as a member of a trade mission. In his *Vermehrten Moscowitischen und Persianischen Reisebeschreibung,* the second edition of which was published in 1656, he described the Âshûrâ celebration he witnessed in 1637 in Ardabîl, the city in Azerbaijan where the Safavid dynasty originated.[7]

"On the fourteenth of May, the Persians started a festival of mourning that lasted ten days, which is why it is referred to with the Arabic word *ashur,* which means ten. It is commemorated each year at the beginning of the month of *Maheram* by the Persians, yet by no other nation of a Muhammadan faith. This *ashur* festival is a commemoration of the memory of Hossein, Aaliy's youngest son, whom they honor as a great imam or saint. He is said to have been slain in the war that *Caliph Yesied* waged against him, first being plagued with great thirst when cut off from the water supply and then wounded with seventy-two arrows, and stabbed by one named *Senan ben*

Anessi, and then utterly killed by Shemr Sültzausen.[8]

"The reason, though, why this festival lasts ten days is because Hossein, who wanted to travel from Medina to Kufa, was followed by his enemy for ten full days, intimidated to death. At the time of these celebrations the Persians wear clothing of mourning, they are distressed, and do not allow a shearing knife, which they normally use daily, to come near their heads. They practice restraint, drink no wine, and survive on water.

"At that time, all of Ardebil was in bustling motion, busy with peculiar ceremonies. All day long the boys went along various roads together, walking with large flags, decorated at the top with opposing snakes, called *eshder*.[9] The boys sat in the doorways of the mestisids,[10] one called out and the others answered, *'Ya Hossein, ya Hossein!'* That means 'O Hossein'; after sunset on all evenings, especially the last three, even the elderly often came together to certain places with tents. They had quite a few hundred lanterns and torches, held bitter oranges on long swaying staffs just like the children of the *abdâls*,[11] formed a circle, and shouted and cried out with mouths wide open and serious gestures, so violently that their faces turned brown.

"They made room for us who came to view the activities and they handed us burning wax lights. When the time came they sang and marched with the flags and torches through the main streets of the city.

"The last day of this festival was closed with a public oration in the morning and a lot of strange ceremonies in the evening. The *parentatio* [funeral address] was held like the one held for Aaliy. The assembly took place in front of the *Mezar* of *Shaykh Sefi*.[12] Then at the pulpit a large flag was held, which had been made by order of *Fattima, Mahumed's* daughter, with a horseshoe at the top like the one on the horse of Abas, Mahumed's father's brother,[13] and which *Shaykh Sedredin, Shaykh Sefi's* son, brought from Medina to Ardebil. This flag, it is said, when Hossein's name is remembered in that oration, moves greatly, but when the words are read that he was injured 72 times and fell from his horse, it is supposed to wave so wildly that it breaks off at the wood at the top and falls. I myself was not there, that I could have seen it, but the Persians told it to me as a true story. The devil is meanwhile very busy in the children of nonbelieving.

"Around midday the Khan welcomed the legates, telling them that they, the Persians, would perform their *ashur* this night (May 24th). If the legates so desired, they could watch their ceremonies, they were kindly invited with the advance remark that according to Muslim law, they would drink no wine, but only water. After sundown, the legates gathered, including the whole committee. The Khan came toward us, received us kindly, and urged us to be seated on chairs draped with beautiful carpets in orderly fashion in front of the gate (because the action itself was to be held on the great market place) on the left side. He himself sat on the ground to the right of the gate, alone. A long table was set up in Persian manner on the ground; there were many porcelain bowls filled with sweet and nice-smelling waters. In front of the table there were large, four foot high brass lamps with large wax candles, as well as lanterns, in which rags drenched with talc and *naft* were burning.[14] Before our common peoples, there were large wooden lamps, each with twenty or thirty wax lights. On the walls they had glued several hundred lamps of limestone so that all of them, filled with talc and tar, gave off large flames. It looked as if the houses were on fire. Across the square there were many lanterns hanging on long ropes. They were covered with all sorts of colored paper and the light shining through played delicately.

"The residents of the city came together in large numbers, some sitting on the ground, some bringing burning lamps and staffs and bitter oranges in their hands. They formed a circle and sang. The matter is as follows: Since there are five large main streets in Ardebil, and each has its own guild, they are in the habit of going around in separate parties. They have different poets (of whom there were many) who lead them in many songs in praise of Aaliy and Hossein. The ones among them who can sing the best get to sing in the presence of the Khan. The street with the best inventions and ways of singing is honored and presented with sweetened water. This is why they came in parties one after another, stood before the Khan and the legates in a proper circle, sang (or rather, shouted) with all their might, for about two hours. Finally, on order of the Khan, they gave their wish to the legates that God gladly wanted to help them come to the king and be welcomed. Among other things, seven young, naked people danced in a separate circle to the left. They were called *tsaktsaku* and their entire bodies from head to toe were blackened and shining, smeared with tar and soot. They had covered only their nakedness and were a terrible sight, painted like young devils. They banged together stones they had in their hands and called out: 'Ya Hossein! Ya Hossein!' This refers to the great sorrow over the innocent death of Hossein, which is why they sometimes also beat their chests with stones. It was supposedly poor people who ran around the market stands, making such a spectacle the whole time of *ashur*, so they would be given alms for the sake of Hossein. They do not go to their homes to sleep at night, but rather they lie down in the ashes in front of the kitchen as a sign of their mourning. Others, like the blackened ones, are supposed to have smeared themselves with red paint, which was to symbolize the blood of the slain Hossein, but we did not actually see them.

"After the end of such events and ceremonies, the *kelbele khan* let many merry fireworks be shown for the pleasure of the legates. This did not occur without the displeasure of many Persians, who believed that such fireworks common only for festivals of happiness and joy did not seem proper at an important festival of mourning; it was certainly only for the sake of the nonbelievers who nevertheless did not think very highly of their saints."

The report by the French traveler Jean-Baptiste Tavernier leads directly to the court of the Shah himself. Tavernier was granted permission to observe the Muharram ceremonies in 1667 that took place in the presence of Shah Safî I on the large Shah square *(Meydân-e Shâh)* in Isfahân. His report of his forty years of travel was published in German *(Vierzig-jährige Reise-Beschreibung)* in 1681 (citations in the following have been translated from this edition). The author started with a detailed discussion of the difference between the Sunni and Shi'i sects and then moved on to a description of the events that took place on the Meydân, observed by the Shah from the terrace of the palace gate, Alî Qapu (called *Dela* by Tavernier[15]).

"I am now going to the Persians' great ceremonial event, namely, the above-mentioned festival to Hocen and Hussein, the sons of Alî. Eight or ten days prior to the celebration, the most zealous blacken their entire body and face and go through the streets totally naked except for a cloth covering their loins. They hold a stone in each hand and bang them together, all the while making very foolish faces and gestures and unceasingly crying out 'Hussein, Hocen, Hocen, Hussein.' They cry with such force that they foam at the mouth. In the evening they are taken in by pious folks and fed well. Throughout these days, once the sun goes down, one sees pulpits set up at all corners of the markets and many intersections, with preachers, whom the people listen to and who prepare them to sanctify this festival. Meanwhile both men and women gather, and people of every age. There is no day in the year that women have better opportunity to go to their lovers than this one.

"I wish to describe this festival as I saw it on July 3, 1667 through the aid of the nazar or chief steward of the royal court, who called the Dutchman and me to the Meydan, just across from the Dela where the king was seated, and gave us a fine place. . . .

"At seven o'clock in the morning, Cha-Sephi *[Shah Safî]*, who later changed his name and is now called Cha-Soliman, was escorted by the lords of his court, and he sat on his throne in the middle of the Dela. But all the lords remained standing. As soon as he was seated, the great Chief Constable appeared, mounted on a beautiful horse and followed by many young gentlemen. They let the masses that had come to celebrate this festival go out so that each one could be shown his proper place. For the king had requested the Chief Constable to be the master of the ceremonies, commanding him to show each one his place, in order to avoid the disorder that in former times often had occured when one quarter of the city, belonging to a certain church [mosque], had tried to take precedence over another . . . ."

"The Chief Constable then let the companies march in and each one had a bier carried by eight to ten men. On each bier was a coffin, three to four shoes high and five to six long. The wood of the bier was adorned with gold and with silver flowers, the coffin itself covered with a silk drape. As soon as the first company was ordered to march in, three properly ornamented saddle horses were led in, with bows and arrows, round shields, and broad daggers hanging at the sides of the saddles.

"When they had come about 100 steps onto the square and came within sight of the king, the three horses were allowed to gallop. The whole company following started to run, dance, and make the coffins burst open. Each one tossed his small skirt, belt, and cap into the air and they placed their fingers in their mouths to whistle more loudly. Others were almost naked, as was described at the beginning of this chapter, holding two stones in their hands, banging them together and shouting 'Hussein, Hocen, Hocen, Hussein' until, as I said, foam started coming from their mouths. After they circled the square three or four times, the other companies were allowed in, each one orderly taking its turn. Each company was preceded by three saddle horses like the ones ridden by the prophets in the skirmish and they all did the same sorts of things as the first. As soon as one company was finished, it was led to a corner to make room for those to come.

"Two further companies went past, each with a funeral bier and a coffin with a child pretending to be dead lying in it. Two children escorted each one, crying and sighing bitterly. These children symbolized the two children of Hussein. For when the prophet was killed, the children were captured by Yezid, Caliph of Baghdad, and killed. Here one could see a large number of whores who join the splendor, crying and hoping their tears will bring them forgiveness for their sins.

"After all the people were in the square, despite good order, as kept by the Chief Constable, many of them beat themselves. They felt it was an honor, especially in the presence of the king, to throw down each other bravely, believing that if they died in this act they would be considered saints, like those who perform such an act to be buried with honor. The Chief Constable saw that the conflict was intensifying and could grow yet larger; he had five elephants led past, which ended the conflict and attracted the attention of the masses. . . .

"At the side of the hall where the king was seated, a small stage was set up about five or six shoes lower than the platform the king was seated upon. It was covered with carpets. In the middle of the stage, there was a large armchair covered with black pile. The mullah sat upon it, surrounded by six other mullahs. The mullah gave a speech about the death of Hussein and Hocen that lasted half an hour. After he was finished, the king let him present the calaat, or royal habit. . . .

"All of this lasted from seven o'clock in the morning until around midday, when the king returned to his harem. The people did not stop here, however, but carried the biers throughout the whole city for the duration of the day. As it happened, whenever two companies met, each wanting to have the upper hand and proceed first, they got caught up with each other and often fought each other down, since they were not begrudged carrying other weapons such as sticks, like levers."

Tavernier is one of the first who described the street fights, in which the processions from the respective parts of the city restaged the battle of Karbalâ. Participants on both sides chanted "Yâ Hussain," plunging themselves into the tumult to demonstrate their readiness to fight for the imam and if necessary even die a martyr's death.

Engelbert Kaempfer of Lemgo, who was in Isfahân in 1684-85 serving as a physician and clerk in a Swedish delegation, reported that "the worst conflicts take place on the anniversary of Hosein's murder. Aroused by the humiliating fate of the Alids, the masses go at each other and bloodily beat each other's heads."[16]

The last report cited here is that of William Francklin, whose *Observations made on a Tour from Bengal to Persia in the Years 1786-7* appeared in 1790.[17]

"The first ten days of the month Mohurrum (being the first of the Mahomedan year) are observed throughout Persia as a solemn mourning; it is called by the natives *Dèha*, or a space of ten days. During this period the Persians, and all the followers of Ali, lament the death of Imaum Hossein, the second son of that prophet, who was slain in the war against Yezzeed, the son of Moaweia, Caliph of the Musselmans. This event happened at a place called Kerbelaiè, which in Persian implies *grief and misfortune*."[18]

Then comes a description of the events at Karbalâ, after which Francklin continues:

"All these various events are represented by the Persians during the first ten days of Mohurrum. On the 27th of the preceding month of Zùlhuj, they erect the *Mumbirs*[19] on the pulpits in the mosques, the insides of which are on this occasion lined with black cloth. On the 1st of Mohurrum the Akhunds, and Peish Numazz's[20] (or Mahomedan priests) mount the pulpits, and begin what is denominated by the Persians *al Wakàa,*[21] or a recital of the life and actions of Ali, and his sons Hussan and Hossein; describing at the same time the circumstances attending the melancholy fate of the Imaum Hossein: the recital is made in a slow solemn tone of voice, and is really affecting to hear, being written with all the pathetic elegance the Persian language is capable of expressing. At intervals the people strike their breasts with violence, weeping bitterly at the same time, and exclaiming, Ah Hossein! ah Hossein! *Heif az Hossein!* Alas

Fig. 6: The deceased al-Qâsim before his wedding chamber
in Karbalâ, presented in a Muharram procession in Shusha
(Nagorno-Karabakh), 1869.

for Hossein!—Other parts of the Wakàa are in verse, which are
sung in cadence to a doleful tune. Each day some particular
action of the story is represented by people selected for the purpose of personating those concerned in it; effigies also are
brought out and carried in procession through the different
neighbourhoods: among these they have one representing the
river Euphrates, which they call *Abi Ferat*. Troops of boys and
young men, some personating the soldiers of Ibn Sa'd, others
those of Hossein and his company, run about the streets, beating and skirmishing with each other, and each have their
respective banners and ensigns of distinction. Another pageant
represents the Caliph Yezzeed seated on a magnificent throne,
surrounded by guards; and by his side is placed the European
ambassador afore-mentioned." As Francklin had explained earlier, the European ambassador happened to be present at the
court of Caliph Yazîd in Damascus when the captured survivors
of Karbalâ—the women and the young, fourth imam Alî Zayn

al-Âbidîn—were presented to the caliph. "[He] was struck with compassion at the miserable appearance they made, and asked Yezzeed who they were; the Caliph replied, that they were of the family of the prophet Mahomed . . . whereupon the ambassador rose up and reviled the Caliph very bitterly for thus treating the family of his own prophet. The haughty Yezzeed, enraged at the affront, ordered the ambassador to go himself and bring him the head of Zein al Abudeen, on pain of immediate death; this, however, the ambassador flatly refused; and, as the Persians believe, embracing the head of Hossein, turned Mussulman; on which he was immediately put to death by the command of Yezzeed."

The story of the Christian (Byzantine) ambassador, whose sympathy was greater than that of the Sunni Yazîd and who became a martyr, has a firm place in the Karbalâ legend. It is often portrayed on pictures and in the passion play. But let us continue with Francklin's report:

"Among the most affecting representations is the marriage of young Càsim [al-Qâsim], the son of Hussun, and nephew of Hossein, with his daughter; but this was never consummated, as Càsim was killed in a skirmish on the banks of the Euphrates, on the 7th of Mohurrum. On this occasion, a boy represents the bride, decorated in her wedding garments, and attended by the females of the family chanting a mournful elegy, in which is related the circumstance of her betrothed husband being cut off by infidels—(for such is the term by which the Sheias speak of the Sunnies). The parting between her and her husband is also represented, when on his going to the field she takes an affectionate leave of him; and, on his quitting her, presents him with a burial vest, which she puts round his neck: at this sight the people break out into the most passionate exclamations of grief and distress, and execrate the most bitter curses upon Yezzeed, and all those who had any concern in destroying the family of their Imaum.

"The sacred pigeons, which are affirmed by the Persians to have carried the news of Hossein's death from Kerbelài to

Medeena (having first dipped their beaks in his blood as a confirmation), are also brought forth on this occasion. The horses on which Hossein and his brother Abbàs are supposed to have rode, are shewn to the people, painted as covered with wounds, and stuck full of arrows.

"During these various processions much injury is often sustained, as the Persians are all frantic even to enthusiasm, and they believe uniformly that the souls of those slain during the Mohurrum will infallibly go that instant into *Paradise;* this, added to their frenzy, which for the time it lasts is such as I never saw exceeded by any people, makes them despise and even court death. Many there are who inflict voluntary wounds on themselves, and some who almost entirely abstain from water during these ten days, in memory of, and as a sufferance for, what their Imaum suffered from the want of that article; and all people abstain from the bath, and even from changing their clothes during the continuance of the *Mohurrum.* On the 10th day, the coffins of those slain in the battle are brought forth, stained with blood on which scymitars and turbans, adorned with herons feathers, are laid:—these are solemnly interred, after which the priests again mount the pulpits and read the Wakàa. The whole is concluded with curses and imprecations on the Caliph Yezzeed.

"The Persians affirm this to be a martyrdom, and throughout the whole of the recital Hossein is distinguished by the appellation of *Sheheed,* or the martyr. They add, that he also knew of, and voluntarily suffered it as an expiation for the sins of all who believe in Ali, and consequently that all who lament the death of their Imaum, shall find favour at the day of judgment: they further assert, that if Hossein had thought proper to make use of the powers of his Imaumship, the whole world could not have hurt him, but that he chose to suffer a voluntary death, that his followers might reap the benefit of it in a future state: whence arises the belief among the Persians, that at the day of judgment Fatima, the wife of Ali, and mother of the two Imaums Hussun and Hossein, will present herself before the throne of

God, with the severed head of Hossein in one hand, and the heart of Hussun (who was poisoned) in the other, demanding absolution in their name for the sins of the followers of Ali; and they doubt not but God will grant their request.—I had these particulars from a religious Persian, and as they are not generally known to Europeans, I have taken the liberty of inserting them."

3. The Elegy

The Âshûrâ ritual is based on lamentation and self-accusation that commemorates the events in Karbalâ and illustrates them through gestures, pictures, and pantomime—and later spoken—dramatic presentations. The Arabic words for the lamentation of the dead are *marthiya* or *nawh,* or *ta'ziya* ("offering condolences"); in Persian it is *nowha* or *mâtam.* Over the course of time, however, these words have taken on special connotations in the various countries in the Shi'i world. In the Arabic and Persian realm, *ta'ziya* refers to the dramatic passion play; in India, on the other hand, it refers to the pictures of coffins and graves that are carried throughout the procession. The Persian *mâtam* is used in India to refer to self-flagellation.[22]

The prototype of the elegy developed at the end of the fifteenth century in Iran. Husayn Wâ'ez Kâshefî is the author of *Garden of the Martyrs (Rawdat ash-shuhadâ');* the Arabic word for "garden" in its Persian pronunciation, *rowza,* has become the name for the entire genre. The reader of such an elegy, the "rowza singer" *(rowza-khân),* can be asked to come into the home. He is one of the few strangers allowed to enter the private section of a residence *(andarûn),* where women are also present. The women also take active part in the performance of the rowza khân.

Adam Olearius witnessed such a recitation in 1637 in

Fig. 7: Rowza recitation in the courtyard of a private home.
The recitor is standing at the stair-shaped pulpit (Rowza Khân).

Shemâkhâ in Azerbaijan, though this particular rowza did not
recall the events of Karbalâ, but the murder of Alî in Kufa:

"The seventh of February or, according to the Persian
almanach the 22nd of Ramesan, is the Ashur, or yearly commemoration of Aaliy, the great saint and patron of the Persians.
The entire city gathers and special ceremonies are held and
great speeches are given in a house built on the outskirts of the
city expressly for this purpose. When we came to observe the
process, the khan, who stood with the calenter and other great
men at the aforementioned house, ordered that space be made
for us to come closer to be able to have a good view of everything. Under a canopy on a chair raised two fathoms high sat
the khathib[23] or *parentator* [funeral speaker] in a blue robe of
mourning, for that which is for us in mourning the color black
is for them blue. He read as if singing with a clear voice and
lively gestures for two hours from a book, *Maktelnameh* [Ara-

bic-Persian *maqtal-nâme*, or 'murder book'], which tells the story of Aaliy's life and death. Around the khathib's chair on the ground sat many pastors, all with white mendils [Arabic: turbans] on their heads, who started singing at different times during the oration. It was done in the following manner: Since the aforementioned book now and then included fine, notable sayings and verses, the orator indicated when they appeared, saying the first words and then becoming silent. Then the familiar odes or songs were sung by the others. After each song one of them called out with a loud voice: *Laanet khuday ber kushendi Aaliy bad!* May he who murdered Aaliy be cursed before God! Then the entire assembly responded: *Bish bad, kem bad.* May that come to be rather more than less!

"When it was read how Aaliy told his children in advance of his demise (many say from the science of astrology, in which he is said to have been very well-versed) and how he indicated his servant, Abdurraman Ibni Meltzem [*Abdurrahmân ibn Muljam*], that it would be done by his hand, and the children told their father with bitter tears that he should be careful and rather kill Abdurraman himself, so that they would not be made into poor orphans through the murder of their father, all the Persians started to cry. And when it was read about the murder itself, that it happened right in the mestzid [*masjid,* mosque] while he was praying, and how after the father's death the children revolted so terribly, most of the people were crying so much that they made loud noises. After the reading ended, the khathib was honored with a new silk gown from the khan, which he had to put on right away. Then three coffins covered with black cloths were led around in a circle; these symbolized the coffins of Aaliy and his two sons, Hassan and Hossein. There were two long crates covered with blue cloths that were supposed to be the repositories of the remaining spiritual books of Aaliy. Also, two beautiful horses with bows, arrows, and exquisite turbans on them; many flags of victory. One person carried a small round tower on a pole. It was called nakhal,[24] and had four sabres stuck into it, which you could hardly see for all the decorations attached to it. Many carried on their heads small houses, or *selle,* covered with colorful, feathered bands, flowers, and other ornaments, in which the opened *Alcoran* was supposed to lie. These hopped and jumped to melancholy music of large cymbals, pipes, tambourines, and army drums. Several groups of boys had long poles, jumping around in separate circles, grabbing each other by the shoulders and shouting, one first and the others responding: *Heyder, Heyder* (that is Aaliy's name),[25] *Hassan, Hossein.* With such ceremonies they then went into the city. On this 21st of Ramesan, when Aaliy is said to have given up his spirit, there are celebrations of great mourning carried out in the above-explained manner throughout all of Persia. Mahumed, said to be their great prophet, is not granted any day of commemoration."[26]

Just as in this case the death of the first imam Alî is celebrated by reciting elegies, the anniversaries of all other martyred imams are also commemorated. Olearius mentioned a special meeting place outside the city that is used specifically for such ceremonies. In Iran these ceremonial halls are called *tekyeh* or *Hoseyniyyeh;* in India they are *Âshûrkhâna.* They are administered in the individual districts of the city by the same guilds, associations, or clubs that also organize the processions. They are not only used to store religious implements, but also as a clubhouse, where recitations, self-flagellation, and passion plays take place. Such tekyehs in Iran are often decorated with series of pictures either painted or on glazed tiles, illustrating the episodes of the passion. The most famous of this type of building is the Hoseiniyya-ye Mushîr in Shîrâz, in which the tympanum over the entrance is covered with paintings. The tekyeh of Mo'âven ol-Molk in Kermânshâh, built in 1917-20, has the most elaborate series of glazed tiles in Iran.

The rowza's recitations are not limited to the passion month of Muharram, nor to the anniversaries of the deaths of the martyred imams. They can take place throughout the entire year for special occasions. A special form is called "curtain hanging" *(pardedârî);* on a large screen about two meters high and four meters wide, the scenes of Karbalâ are painted, entirely filling the picture, leaving no empty spaces. In the center there is usually an oversized al-Husayn on his horse, splitting the head of an adversary with his sword. Like a minstrel, the speaker recites the scenes of the passion as he points to the corresponding illustrations with a pointer and explains them.

4. The Ten Days of Muharram

The climax of the Shi'i festival calendar are the first ten days of the first month of the Islamic year, Muharram. Since the Islamic lunar year is eleven days shorter than the solar calendar commonly used, all dates shift eleven days from one year to the next with respect to our calendar. Consequently, holiday

Fig. 8: Âshûrâ procession in Tehran (1993): Standard *('alam)* with the names of the twelve imams.

months such as Ramadân or Muharram are not bound to any particular season and all Islamic holidays move backwards throughout the solar year.

The ten-day Muharram rites commemorate the time when Imam al-Husayn and his small army were blocked at the plain of Karbalâ by the troops of the governor of Kufa. Each of the ten festival days focuses on a different episode of the passion story. The recitations, processions with emblems and standards (alam) or tableaux vivants (living pictures), and the performances of the passion play follow the prescribed order of the historical events. From the first to the third of Muharram, Husayn's arrival in Karbalâ and his futile negotiations with Caliph Yazîd's representatives are the subject of the presentations. On the fourth, Hurr at-Tamîmî's martyrdom is commemorated. At-Tamîmî was the commander of the opposing cavalry who plays the role of the "remorseful thief" in the Shi'i passion play. He regrets his sin, goes over to Husayn's side and finds his death at the side of the Imam. On the fifth, the martyrdom of Aun and Muhammad, the young sons of al-Husayn's sister Zaynab, are lamented. The sixth of Muharram is the day commemorating al-Husayn's oldest son, eighteen-year-old Alî al-Akbar, who was killed while supporting his father, dying in his arms. In some places, this day also includes commemoration of the Imam's youngest son, the infant Alî al-Asghar, who died from an arrow shot through his throat. In his memory, a cradle is often carried in the processions on this day.[27] Young al-Qâsim ibn al-Hasan is remembered on the 7th of Muharram. He was the unfortunate bridegroom who fell on the day he married the daughter of his uncle, al-Husayn (see figure 6 on p. 54). The 8th is the day of commemoration of al-Abbâs, the Imam's half-brother whose arms were cut off while attempting to fetch water from the Euphrates for the parched martyrs. The "ninth" (Tâsû'â) and "tenth" (Âshûrâ) are the climax of the celebrations, commemorating the death of al-Husayn himself. Flagellants and sword scourgers usually do not appear until these days.

Municipal associations organize these ceremonies and processions. In principle they function the same, whether in the Lebanese city of an-Nabatiyya, the Iraqi al-Kâzimiyya, throughout Iran, or in Hyderabad, India.[28]

5. The Passion Play

The Arabic word *ta'ziya* actually means "offering condolences" and originally referred to the all of the Âshûrâ rituals. In Iran (pronounced there as *ta'ziyat* or *ta'ziyeh*) it has evolved to mean the passion play, in which the events of Karbalâ are dramatically performed in scenes with dialogue. In India, on the other hand, this word is used for the coffins carried in the processions.

The Âshûrâ ritual celebrations already included dramatic elements as early as the tenth century in Baghdad. Tents were pitched to symbolize al-Husayn's camp. Passers-by and spectators were asked for a sip of water to commemorate the thirst suffered by the martyrs (see above, p. 43-44). Travelogues from the Safavid period (1501-1722) often spoke of objects that were carried and "living" images—for example, of the dead children in their coffins. There is no documented evidence of actual dramas with spoken dialogue during the Safavid dynasty. Apparently, the ta'ziyeh first emerged in the eighteenth century in Iran. William Francklin's report, cited above (see p. 53-57), of his journey to Iran in 1786-87 is the earliest evidence of dramatic elements.

The Englishman James Morier, who traveled through the Near East from India to Constantinople from 1810 to 1816, was the first European to report in detail on the ta'ziyeh:[29]

"The tragical termination of [al-Husayn's] life, commencing with his flight from Medina, and terminating with his death on the plain of Kerbelah, has been drawn up in the form of a drama, consisting for several parts, of which one is performed by actors on each successive day of the mourning. . . .

"The preparations which were made throughout the city consisted in erecting large tents, that are there called *takieh*,[30] in the streets and open places, in fitting them up with black linen, and furnishing them with objects emblematical of the mourning. These tents are erected either at the joint expence of the *mahal*, or district, or by men of consequence, as an act of devotion; and all ranks of people have a free access to them. The expense of a takieh consists in the hire of a mollah, or priest, of actors and their clothes, and in the purchase of lights. Many there are who seize this opportunity of atoning for past sins, or of rendering thanks to heaven for some blessing, by adding charity to the good act of erecting a takieh, and distribute gratuitous food to those who attend it.

"Our neighbour Mahomed Khan had a takieh in his house, to which all the people of the mahal flocked in great numbers. During the time of this assemblage we heard a constant noise of drums, cymbals, and trumpets. We remarked that besides the takiehs in different open places and streets of the town, a wooden pulpit, without any appendage, was erected, upon which a mollah was mounted, preaching to the people who were collected around him . . . . An European Ambassador who is said to have intrigued with Yezid in favour of Hossein, is brought forwards accordingly to be an actor in one of the parts of the tragedy, and the populace were in consequence inclined to look favourably upon us.[31] Notwithstanding the excitation of the public mind, we did not cease to take our usual rides, and we generally passed unmolested through the middle of congregations, during the time of their devotions.

"Such little scruples have they at our seeing their religious ceremonies, that on the 8th night of the Moharrem, the Grand Vizier invited the whole of the Embassy to attend his takieh. On entering the room we found a large assembly of Persians clad in dark-coloured clothes, which, accompanied with their black caps, their black beards, and their dismal faces, really looked as if they were *afflicting their souls*. We observed, that *no man did put on his ornaments* (Ex. 33,4). They neither wore their dag-

gers, nor any parts of their dress which they look upon as orna-
mental. A mollah of high consideration sat next to the Grand
Vizier, and kept him in serious conversation, whilst the remaining part of the society communicated with each other in whis-
pers. After we had sat some time, the windows of the room in
which we were seated were thrown open, and we then discovered a priest placed on a high chair, under the covering of a
tent, surrounded by a crowd of the populace; the whole of the
scene being lighted up with candles. He commenced by an
exordium, in which he reminded them of the great value of each
tear shed for the sake of Imâm Hossein, which would be an
atonement for a past life of wickedness; and also informed them
with much solemnity, that *whatsoever soul it be that shall not
be afflicted in the same day, shall be cut off from among the people.* Lev. 23,29. He then began to read from a book with a sort
of nasal chaunt, that part of the tragic history of Hossein
appointed for the day, which soon produced its effect upon his
audience, for he scarcely had turned over three leaves, before
the Grand Vizier commenced to shake his head to and fro, to
utter in a most piteous voice the usual Persian exclamation of
grief, *"wahi! wahi! wahi!"* both of which acts were followed in a
more or less violent manner by the rest of the audience. The
chaunting of the priest lasted nearly an hour, and some parts of
his story were indeed pathetic, and well calculated to rouse the
feelings of a superstitious and lively people. In one part of it, all
the company stood up, and I observed that the Grand Vizier
turned himself towards the wall, with his hand extended before
him, and prayed. After the priest had finished, a company of
actors appeared, some dressed as women, who chaunted forth
their parts from slips of paper, in a sort of recitativo, that was
not unpleasing even to our ears. In the very tragical parts, most
of the audience appeared to cry very unaffectedly; and as I sat
near the Grand Vizier, and to his neighbour the priest, I was
witness to many real tears that fell from them. In some of these
mournful assemblies, it is the custom for a priest to go about to
each person at the height of his grief, with a piece of cotton in

his hand, with which he carefully collects the falling tears, and which he then squeezes into a bottle, preserving them with the greatest caution. This practically illustrates that passage in the 56th Psalm, 8, *Put thou my tears into thy bottle.* Some Persians believe, that in the agony of death, when all medicines have failed, a drop of tears so collected, put into the mouth of a dying man, has been known to revive him; and it is for such use, that they are collected.

"On the Rooz Catl [Persian *rûz-e qatl:* day of the murder], the tenth day, the Ambassador was invited by the King to be present at the termination of the ceremonies, in which the death of Hossein was to be represented. We set off after breakfast, and placed ourselves in a small tent, that was pitched for our accommodation, over an arched gateway, which was situated close to the room in which His Majesty was to be seated.

"We looked upon the great *maidan,* or square, which is in front of the palace, at the entrance of which we perceived a circle of Cajars, or people of the King's own tribe,[32] who were standing barefooted, and beating their breasts in cadence to the chaunting of one who stood in the centre, and with whom they now and then joined their voices in chorus. *Smiting the breast* (St. Luke 18,13) is an universal act throughout the mourning; and the breast is made bare for that purpose, by unbuttoning the top of the shirt. The King in order to show his humility, ordered the Cajars, among whom were many of his own relations, to walk about without either shoes or stockings, to superintend the order of the different ceremonies about to be performed; and they were to be seen stepping tenderly over the stones, with sticks in their hands doing the duties of menials, now keeping back a crowd, then dealing out blows with their sticks, and settling the order of the processions.

"Part of the square was partitioned off by an enclosure, which was to represent the town of Kerbelah, near which Hossein was put to death; and close to this were two small tents, which were to represent his encampment in the desert with his family. A wooden platform covered with carpets, upon which the actors were to perform, completed all the scenery used on the occasion.

"A short time after we had reached our tent, the King appeared; and although we could not see him, yet we were soon apprised of his presence by all the people standing up, and by the bowing of his officers. The procession then commenced as follows:—

"First came a stout man, naked from the waist upwards, balancing in his girdle a long thick pole, surmounted by an ornament made of tin, curiously wrought with devices from the Koran, in height altogether about thirty feet.

"Then another, naked like the former, balanced an ornamented pole in his girdle still more ponderous, though not so high, upon which a young dervish, resting his feet upon the bearer's girdle had placed himself, chaunting verses with all his might in praise of the King.

"After him a person of more strength, and more nakedness, a water carrier, walked forwards, bearing an immense leather sack filled with water slung over his back, on which by way of bravado four boys were piled one over the other. This personage, we were told, was emblematical of the great thirst which Hossein suffered in the desert.

"A litter in the shape of a sarcophagus, which was called the *Caber Peighember,* or the tomb of the prophet [Persian *qabr-e peighamber],* succeeded, borne on the shoulders of eight men. On its front was a large oval ornament entirely covered with precious stones, and just above it, a great diamond star. On a small projection were two tapers placed on candlesticks enriched with jewels. The top and sides were covered with Cashmerian shawls, and on the summit rested a turban, intended to represent the head-dress of the prophet. On each side walked two men bearing poles, from which a variety of beautiful shawls were suspended, at the top of which were representations of Mahomed's hand, studded with jewellery.

"After this came four led horses, caparisoned in the richest manner. The fronts of their heads were ornamented with plates, entirely covered with diamonds, that emitted a thousand beautiful rays. Their bodies were dressed with shawls and gold stuffs; and on their saddles were placed some object emblematical of the death of Hossein. When all these had passed, they arranged themselves in a row to the right of the King's apartment.

"After a short pause, a body of fierce-looking men, with only a loose white sheet thrown over their naked bodies, marched forwards. They were all begrimmed with blood; and each brandishing a sword, they sang a sort of hymn, the tones of which were very wild. These represented the sixty-two relations, or the martyrs as the Persians call them, who acompanied Hossein, and were slain in defending him. Close after them was led a white horse, covered with artificial wounds, with arrows stuck all about him, and caparisoned in black, representing the horse upon which Hossein was mounted when he was killed. A band of about fifty men, striking two pieces of wood together in their hands, completed the procession. They arranged themselves in rows before the King, and marshalled by a *maître de ballet,* who stood in the middle to regulate their movements, they performed a dance, clapping their hands in the best possible time. The *maître de ballet* all this time sang in recitativo, to which the dancers joined at different intervals with loud shouts and reiterated clapping of their pieces of wood.

"The procession were succeeded by the tragedians. Hossein came forwards, followed by his wives, sisters, and relatives. They performed many long and tedious acts; but as our distance from the stage was too great to hear the many affecting things which no doubt they said to each other, we will proceed at once to where the unfortunate Hossein lay extended on the ground, ready to receive the death-stroke from a ruffian dressed in armour, who acted the part of executioner. At this moment a burst of lamentation issued from the multitude, and heavy sobs and real tears came from almost every one of those who were near enough to come under our inspection. The indignation of the populace wanted some object upon which to vent itself, and it fell upon those of the actors who had performed the parts of

Yezid's soldiers. No sooner was Hossein killed, than they were driven off the ground by a volley of stones, followed by shouts of abuse. We were informed that it is so difficult to procure performers to fill these characters, that on the present occasion a party of Russian prisoners were pressed into the army of Yezid, and they made as speedy an exit after the catastrophe, as it was in their power.

"The scene terminated by the burning of Kerbelah. Several reed huts had been constructed behind the enclosure before mentioned, which of a sudden were set on fire. The tomb of Hossein was seen covered with black cloth, and upon it sat a figure disguised in a *tiger's* skin, which was intended to represent the miraculous *lion,* recorded to have kept watch over his remains after he had been buried. The most extraordinary part of the whole exhibition was the representation of the dead bodies of the martyrs; who having been decapitated, were all placed in a row, each body with a head close to it. To effect this, several Persians buried themselves alive, leaving the head out just above round; whilst others put their heads under ground, leaving out the body. The heads and bodies were placed in such relative positions to each other, as to make it appear that they had been severed. This is done by way of penance; but in hot weather the violence of the exertion has been known to produce death. The whole ceremony was terminated by the *khotbeh* [Arabic *khutba:* sermon], which is an action of prayer for Mahomed, his descendants, and for the prosperity of the King."

Reports of the ta'ziyeh became more and more frequent in the nineteenth century. The most detailed description of the passionate theater of the Persians was written by Count Arthur de Gobineau, a French diplomat who spent three years in Iran from 1855-1858, excerpted following:

"The passion for the theater is shared by the entire nation. Men, women, and children all become totally caught up in it, and such a spectacle brings out the whole city. A more or less large shelter is set up for this purpose on all squares in all dis-

tricts. Several persons of the drama stand underneath it, but
most of the action takes place on the square itself, at the same
level as the spectators. The women crowd together on one side
and the men on the other, but the two groups are not separated
all too strictly. The performance is always about a drama from
the life of the Persians, a story of persecution by the Abbasid
caliphs. The most well-known of these is the one performed during the month of Moharrem, dealing with the death of Aly's sons
and their families on the plains of Kerbéla. The performance
continues for ten days, each day's presentation lasting three or
four hours. The plays are lyrical pieces, extremely beautiful and
emotional. Each one takes up where the previous one leaves off
and they are told with much passion. No length is spared, and
the Persians never get their fill of the detailed description of the
suffering, need, fear, and fright experienced by their favorite
saints. The entire assembly sobs, one louder than the next,
emitting cries of deep affliction. These responses are for the
most part genuine, for it is indeed difficult not to be moved, and
I have even seen Europeans who have been overcome with sorrow. Some are obviously hypocrites, and they are by no means
the most quiet ones.

"From time to time the mullah, who is seated opposite upon
a raised chair, speaks to the crowd, explaining how much the
imams suffered. He also goes into considerable detail about
their anguish, paraphrasing the drama, and cursing the tyrannical caliph, and he invokes prayer. At the same time the crowd,
at least the women, start violently beating their chests in
cadence, chanting a kind of antiphonal song and screaming
wildly and unceasingly 'Husseyn, Hassan!' After this intermezzo the play continues. Even though the story has remained the
same over many years, each time something is changed, and in
general, the emotional pieces are expanded and developed further. It is beautiful how the actors who play the hated roles, at
the thought of their own villainy, shed just as many tears as the
audience. I observed one man who played the despised role of
Yézyd. He was so indignant with himself that he sobbed uncon-

Fig. 9: Performance of a ta'ziyeh in a village (1860-61).

trollably while spewing forth the hideous threats against the saints Hassan and Husseyn and he could hardly speak, which pushed the emotions of the crowd to their peak."[33]

At the end of his book *Les religions et les philosophies dans l'Asie centrale*, Gobineau dedicated several extensive chapters to the ta'ziyeh and included the first translation of *The Marriage of Qâsim.*[34]

Figure 9, depicting a ta'ziyeh performance, was taken from the report by Heinrich Brugsch on the Royal Prussian legation to Persia (1860-61).[35] It shows the performers, including a number of children, with their scripts in their hands. Up to the present day it is common practice for actors to read their lines; the dramatic director—often the author—is frequently present, whispering lines and instructions during the scene, without this breaking the illusion for the audience.

French archaeologist Jane Dieulafoy traveled through western Iran in 1881-82. Disguised as a man and accompanied by

Fig. 10: Ta'ziyeh performance in Qazvîn (Iran) in 1881.

her husband, she surveyed ancient monuments. Figure 10 on page 72 was taken from her travel log, as was the following description of a ta'ziyeh performance in Qazvîn, northwest of Tehran:

"May 12. Today, Friday, I was going for a walk in the outlying districts when the sound of a brass instrument penetrated my ear. A large crowd had gathered at a square a long way off from the caravan routes. The audience was watching the performance of a religious tragedy about the death of Ali's sons, Hassan and Houssein, who had been killed at the behest of the caliphs. These dramas are peculiar to the Shi'a sect. During their days of mourning, when the Iranians hear the story of the martyrs of their faith, their passions get inflamed to a most vehement hatred of the Sunnis, who committed the massacre of the legitimate heirs of Mahomet.

"There is no hall in Kazbin like the one in Teheran where a dazzling performance could take place. The spectators squat on their heels gathered around an open square reserved for the performers. On one side are the veiled women and on the other, the men with round peasant's caps on their heads. The only accessories are a carpet laid out on the ground with a sabre and a pitcher of water on it. The deep blue of the sky serves as the backdrop and a brilliant sun is the pale, hazy lighting of our theater. Two children wearing huge green turbans play the role of the ancient choir of Greek tragedies and they declaim songs of lamentation in a musical rhythm that draws tears from all the spectators. During the most emotional moments, the sobs of the actors join those of the crowd, and even the traitor, whose face is covered by a hood, cries and wails on account of his villainy and the injustice he committed. The women let out cries of pain and words of sympathy for the victims; they beat their chests and shoulders, and once they have sufficiently drawn out these expressions of emotion and sympathy, they suddenly calm down and resume the cheerful conversations they had interrupted only moments earlier. The orchestra, made up of a drum and a trumpet, stands at the corner of the carpet and intensifies the pious howling of the audience with dissonant accents. Not far off, a large man sitting on a wooden throne displays the satisfaction of an impresario presenting the audience with a first-class troupe."[36]

Roy Mottahedeh, the author of one of the best books on the spiritual world of the Iranian Shi'ites, made the following remarks concerning the ta'ziyeh:

"Usually the heroes speak verse, the villains prose; the protagonists wear green and white, the antagonists wear red. For the last few generations warriors have worn British officers' jackets instead of coats of mail, and for over a century one of the stock plays revolves around the 'Ambassador of the Europeans,' who, with magnificent disregard for chronology, appears at the court of Yazid, the oppressor of Hosain, in order to plead for his life. Learned characters often wear reading glases and, recently, bad characters wear sunglasses.

"In fact, the passion play, or *taaziyeh,* is not—and in no sense wants to be—illusionistic theater. A bowl of water represents the Euphrates; if the angel Gabriel carries an umbrella, the audience knows he has just descended from heaven. . . . It is exactly the community of emotion and the absence of any fixed barrier between the actors and the audience that give these plays their force; actors and audience flow over one another the way text and miniature flow onto each other in a Persian manuscript. Nowadays when the marriage is performed in the play about Qasem which Francklin described two hundred years ago, cookies are passed among the audience while festive music is played. Then suddenly the riderless horse of Hosain's eldest son [Alî al-Akbar], who has been defending the small band during the marriage, enter the joyous scene. Everyone freezes in position. Qasem passes through the audience (since this is theater in the round) to reach 'the battlefield,' and he quickly returns at the head of a procession that carries the slain son of Hosain on shields. The whole audience rises to its feet and weeps, as at a real funeral procession. And, as it is a mark of respect to the deceased to carry the coffin, even those far from the procession raise their hands in the air as if to support it. The body is laid on the stage, and funeral music is played while the exuberant wedding music is resumed. The audience finds itself both laughing and weeping as the conflicting scenes continue onstage. Throughout these proceedings the director has been walking around the stage reciting bits of narrative and beating his breast with emotion at moments of sadness.

". . . . The actors are not supposed to 'identify' with the persons they represent; in any case, to do so is theologically forbidden, although it is widely believed that only a good person can play Hosain effectively and only a bad man can make a convincing Shemr, the killer of Hosain. Instead the actors and the audience share in a joy and a horror that such events took place; in fact, some actors describe themselves as transformed by the emotion of the audience. The emotion of the audience is called forth by signals indicating the emotional content of the events portrayed. And since this is not a theater of suspense, since everyone knows the events in advance, the climaxes do not necessarily come when crucial events occur; they come when crucial signals appear. The climax of the play on Ashura does not occur when Hosain is killed onstage; it occurs when he puts on his white shroud. Hosain has gone to Kerbela knowing of the prophesies that he would be killed there; as he says in one play, 'Men travel by night and their destinies travel toward them.' The crowning symbol of his choice of martyrdom is that he puts on his own shroud. Emotions of horror and sorrow reach a climax not because the audience has 'empathy' for the 'character' the actor portrays but because they feel the drama of the role of martyrdom of which he reminds them."[37]

Gobineau had also seen the melodrama of the "Frankish" ambassador—in the legend he was actually an ambassador of the Byzantine emperor Johannes at the court of the Caliph of Damascus:

"We Frenchmen have the honor of playing a wonderful role in the performance about the death of the imam, the son of Aly. An ambassador of King John (Which King John? That is not easy to say) was at the court of Caliph Yézyd when the arrival of the members of the holy family captured at Kerbéla was announced. He sought to convince the tyrant to show favor on these women and children. When his efforts proved futile, he was so impassioned that he declared himself a Muslim and a Shi'ite, and suffered a martyr's death. One can imagine the light in which we are seen due to this event."[38] The actors of the royal tekyeh in Tehran sometimes chose to borrow uniforms from European diplomats for this piece in order to properly depict the Frankish ambassador and his entourage. This practice was documented in pictorial representations of the "passion" episodes, which are often nothing more than pictorial renditions of the dramatic scenes. On the large tile painting in the Kermânshâh tekyeh, created around 1920 by a Tehran artist who had evidently seen performances in the state theater

Fig. 11: The prisoners before Caliph Yazîd in Damascus;
in the upper left, the Byzantine delegation
(in uniforms of French and British diplomats).

(tekyeh-ye doulat) in the capital, Caliph Yazîd is shown sitting
on his throne smoking a cigarillo, which was used to symbolize
his depravedness (a detail that also appears in the script
books). The Byzantine ambassador and his attaché are sitting
to his right in the uniforms of British and French diplomats
when the captured women and the young, fourth imam, the

only male survivor of the massacre, are brought in.

The nineteenth century was the heyday of the ta'ziyeh, which experienced its acme around the time Gobineau was in Iran (1855-1858), even though—according to available sources—it had emerged only a mere sixty years earlier. After traveling to England in 1873, Shah Nâsir ad-Dîn was so impressed by a concert he had attended in London's Albert Hall that he had a "state theater" built in Tehran for ta'ziyeh performances. It was a kind of amphitheater equipped with a tent dome that provided protection from the sun. Towards the end of the century, every larger city in Iran had a permanent venue for the ta'ziyeh.

The Persian passion play suffered a hard blow when it was prohibited by the first Pahlavî ruler, Riza Khan *(Reza Shah)* (1925-1941). Similar to Kemal Atatürk in Turkey, Reza Shah tried to eliminate any and all religious influence on public life; to this end he prohibited all Âshûrâ rituals. The processions and ta'ziyeh performances could only be held in secret. Davoud Monchi-Zadeh, who published one of the first modern studies on the ta'ziyeh in 1967, recalled:

"In the summer of 1932 I had the opportunity to see one of the last traces of ta'ziya in the vicinity of Teheran at the grave of Ibn Bâbôye.[39] It was a short play named *Ta'ziya i Alî-Akbar*. It was performed by a couple boys and quite a few men. A relatively small audience had gathered in the courtyard of the shrine around the scattered bundle of rags of the actors, in which their costumes and other paraphernalia were hidden. Since each one played a number of roles, they changed their costumes outside the circle of spectators. A wretched-looking boy who played the role of Alî-Akbar sang with such emotion that people standing near me broke into tears. All of a sudden someone said that a police officer from far away was present. There was a chaotic muddle; the actors in their costumes disappeared behind the trees. In a way, the policeman embodied the evil power (Yazîd's supporters) and the performers were the holy family; it was like a second Karbalâ."[40]

Once Reza Shah was forced to abdicate by the British in 1941, Muharram rituals revived in Iran, but the ta'ziyeh never fully recovered from the decades-long interruption and it never regained the significance it once had in Iran. Not only the reforming rulers but the Shi'i clergy as well had become mistrustful of theater.

"The mullahs remained uncertain about how to evaluate this theater of folk mystical experience. Some condoned it as a powerful means to remind the masses of the meaning of Hosain's mission, for did not the Lord of the Martyrs say, 'I am killed so that they will weep'? Others condemned it as a crude attempt to represent people so sanctified that any representation of them would falsify and thereby do them a dishonor."[41] In present-day Iran the ta'ziyeh—or what is left of it—is at best tolerated, though it can be viewed on the streets and squares even in Tehran. Recently, students of Tehran University have taken up the tradition and perform ta'ziyeh plays on campus—a outlet for creativity and imagination, which they otherwise have very limited opportunities to express.

6. Chest beaters and flagellants

"During the ten days of Moharrem, the entire nation is in mourning. The king, the ministers, the officials all dress in black or gray. Almost everyone else as well. But the masses are not content with this common mourning. The Persians' shirts button down the right side, unlike the European or Arabic style of opening down the middle of the chest. At this time, they wear their shirts open so that the skin is revealed, as this is a symbol of great sorrow. One sees the mule-drivers, the soldiers, the ferrashes [Arabic and Persian: lackeys] with a dagger at their sides, caps on their heads, walking around with open shirts and exposed chests. They curve their right hands into a bowl-like shape and fiercely pound themselves in cadence under the left shoulder. It makes a dull sound that can be heard from a long distance off and sounds very impressive when produced by many hands. This sound is the accompaniment to the brotherhood's singing, the obligatory intermezzo of the ta'ziyeh. Sometimes the blows are heavy and spaced far apart, seeming to make the rhythm slow and lethargic; sometimes they are short and rapid, exciting the spectators. Once the brotherhoods start, it is virtually inevitable that most of the spectators, especially the women, copy their actions. When the leader of the brotherhood gives a signal, all the members start chanting, beating themselves and jumping in place. In short or long intervals, they shout 'Hassan! Housseïn! Hassan! Housseïn!' in short, abrupt tones."

This description of the ritual of the chest beaters (Persian *sîna-zan)* was taken once again from Count Gobineau.[42] The early reports by the Ottoman ambassador, Adam Olearius, and William Francklin (cited here, pp. 45-60) mentioned the chest beaters; chest beating *(sîna-zanî)* was evidently one of the earliest Muharram rituals. It is also a ritual that all followers can practice, including the elderly, women, and children, and even the mullahs. Aside from this basic gesture expressing *mea culpa* (I am guilty), there is an intensified form, as described by Gobineau, that can be practiced only by strong, usually young men. There are various techniques, such as the one-handed method (Persian *yak dast)* with the right hand, or the two-fisted technique *(dô dast).* The latter, also called the "Persian" method *(ajamî),* involves the penitents alternately raising their two arms over their heads and letting them fall with full force onto their chests. Pinault, who observed the rituals in Hyderabad, India, and Gobineau both mentioned the echoing sound that could be heard a long way off. Thomas Lyell, British District Magistrate in Baghdad at the end of World War I, remarked that the dull thud of the breast beating in an-Najaf could be heard on still nights in the desert over a distance of three miles.[43] In April 1993 I witnessed chest beating in the courtyard of the shrine at Qom. The group consisted of approx-

Fig. 12: Muharram procession in 1869 in Shusha
(Nagorno-Karabakh): sword flagellants and chest scourgers.

imately a dozen, thin but strong elderly men in black kimonos
carrying out a two-handed *sîna-zanî* to the performance of a
singer. The blows echoed from under the arch of the court
arcade, where they had situated themselves for the best effect.
Such presentations, which usually last between thirty minutes
and one hour, require a considerable amount of physical
strength, especially since the chest beaters respond at the same
time to the precentor. Hence, this intensive form of *sîna-zanî* is
usually reserved for the men, normally younger ones who actually develop an athletic ambition in this "sport."[44]

Gobineau described the performance of a group of brotherhoods characterized by Persians as "Berbers" *(berberî),* as follows:

"They carry iron chains and pointed needles in their hands.
Some of them have a wooden disc in each hand. They enter the
tekyeh in a procession and start singing—at first slowly—a
litany that consists only of two names: Hassan! Houssein!

Hassan! Houssein! They accompany the tambourine with faster and faster blows. Those who are carrying the discs bang them together in time and everyone starts to dance. The spectators accompany them by pounding their chests in the manner described above. After a short time, the Berbers start scourging themselves with their chains, at first lightly and with obvious caution. Then they become excited and beat themselves more firmly. Those carrying needles start sticking themselves in the arms and cheeks. Blood starts flowing, the crowd becomes frenzied and starts sobbing; the arousal intensifies but when it threatens to get out of hand, the leader of the brotherhood—who hurries among the ranks, spurring the weaker ones on, and holding the arms of those raving excessively—suddenly orders the music to halt and stops the whole event. It is hard not to become caught up in such a scene. One feels sympathy, compassion, horror all at the same time. At the moment the dance ends you can sometimes see how the Berbers raise their arms, wrapped in chains, toward the sky and with a deep voice and an overbearing and confident gaze, they yell out *Ya Allah*, so that you freeze out of sheer amazement; that's how greatly their entire being is transformed."[45]

Gobineau's sharp eye registered that this scourging is monitored strictly, especially when younger boys participate. Great attention is paid to prevent them from seriously injuring themselves and nowadays, an ambulance is generally nearby.[46] It is a false rumor often spread by Europeans that their frenzy can become dangerous for bystanders. Foreign, even non-Muslim spectators are admitted and usually even warmly welcomed. The Muharram ceremonies only become violent when Shi'ites feel provoked by Sunni or Hindu disrupters.

The bloody rituals are usually reserved for the last three days of the ten-day Muharram celebration. It is a privilege for younger men, clubs, and brotherhoods, who do penitence and gain merit in the name of the entire Shi'i community. In addition to the chain flagellants (Persian *zanjîr-zan),* sword or dagger scourgers *(tîgh-zan)* also perform, bloodily beating their

Fig. 13: Chain flagellants.
The man in the center is reading from the Quran.

brows. They wear white shrouds to demonstrate their willingness to be martyred. Younger boys often participate in the flagellation, though they are closely monitored. Most of the martyrs of Karbalâ were, after all, children and adolescents. Women, on the other hand, rarely participate in the bloody self-
mortification and in fact, their participation is generally prohibited.[47]

Mullahs do not scourge themselves either. The ecstatic ritual
is foreign to the realm of the canonists and legal scholars.
According to the *shari'a,* besmirching oneself with blood makes
one impure, and some mullahs view such a ritualistic besmirching with blood as a perversion. Pinault reported of Âyatollâh
Abu'l-Qâsim, son of Iraqi Grand Âyatollâh Khû'î, who went to
India to levy taxes from the Shi'i community. After each visit to
an Âshûrkhâna he supposedly hurried home to perform ritual
washings and thus cleanse himself of the stains from the blood
of the flagellants.[48] Over and over again, Shi'i scholars issue

authoritative legal opinions *(fatwâ)*, opposing the permissibili-
ty of flagellation. They see it as an inadmissable "innovation"
(bid'a), which is just short of "heresy" in Islam.[49] On the other
hand, many mullahs were raised with the centuries-old tradition in their communities and they view the bloody ritual as
something very normal, even commendable. In present-day
Iran, bloody flagellations—and passion plays—are not expressly prohibited, but they are frowned upon and tacitly tolerated.
The revolutionary regime prefers to channel religious enthusiasm for its own purposes. Procession participants flagellate
themselves in a more symbolic fashion, with clothing on their
backs and a scourge of small chains (see figs. 13 and 14).

David Pinault surveyed Shi'i flagellants in Hyderabad about
their reasons for scourging themselves. "We feel it our duty to
shed our blood on Ashura. To prove we are with him, with
Hazrat Imam Husain, we shed our blood, we use implements
and cut ourselves." Someone told a story to justify the bloody
ritual: When the fourth imam, Alî Zayn al-Âbidîn, son of al-
Husayn, lay sick in a tent near Karbalâ, so that he could not
participate in the battle, his father said to him, "When you get
to Medina, tell my followers: The Imam says, 'I missed you—
where were you?'" The flagellation, according to the storyteller,
". . . is a form of response to this last call of Hazrat Imam
Husain, to show that if we had been there at Karbala we would
have stood with him and shed our blood and died with him."
Such statements clearly demonstrate the element of penitence
for the collective failure of the Shi'a, as mentioned above. It is
combined with penitence for individual sins: flagellation "opens
your eyes; it awakens you to your sins of the past year, as you
think about the *Ma'sumin* [Infallible Ones] and compare them
with yourself and the way you've been acting in your sinfulness." Among younger people, flagellation also has definite
characteristics resembling a masculinity ritual. The communi-
ty-promoting strength of the ritual cannot be overlooked. It
bonds the participants into a kind of blood brotherhood; in fact,
it serves to define the community itself. "We do *matam* not just

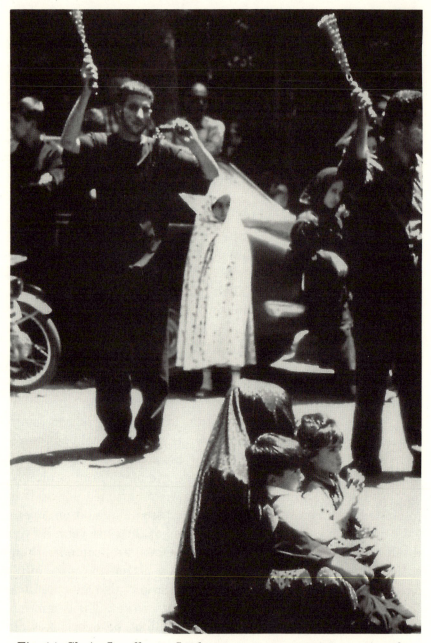

Fig. 14: Chain flagellants. In the center, a woman is accepting the blessing of the act of penance for her children (Tehran 1993).

to commemorate Hazrat Imam Husain but as a way of saying we are Shi'ites."[50]

Shi'i flagellants thus have similar motivations as Christian flagellants, whose earliest documented processions took place in 1260 in central Italy. They soon spread throughout Europe, reaching their peak in 1348-49 during the Black Death. Preachers of repentance such as St. Nicholas of Tolentino (died 1305) in Italy and St. Vincent Ferrer (died 1419) in Spain were a powerful impetus to the movement. The flagellants did not repent for their individual guilt alone, but for the sins of the entire church, especially the sins of the clergy, as the plague was believed to be brought on as their punishment. No wonder the church prohibited flagellation as early as 1349 and then definitively in 1417 at the Council of Constance. Nevertheless, the movement was later revived, especially in the age of the Counter-Reformation. It has continued to survive within the realm of Spanish Catholicism—not only on the Iberian Peninsula, but in Central America and extending as far north as New Mexico.[51] The Holy Week plays a similar role in these areas as Âshûrâ does for the Shi'ites.

Readiness to seek repentance and passion are inextricably linked to one another in the ritual of self-flagellation and they make up the actual core of Shi'i piety. Sinful Shi'ites are seen as worthy of death and only their death can expiate their guilt. Flagellation serves to ritualize the self-sacrifice that is due; it thus becomes repeatable—and surviveable. Believers of the faith do not only confirm their readiness to shed their blood and sacrifice their lives; rather, a portion of the believer's blood is truly shed. Part of the guilt is thus expiated and the believers are then permitted to live another year—until the next Âshûrâ.

PART THREE

The Government of the Expert
The Islam of the Mullahs

1. The Representative of the Hidden Imam

The legitimate leader *(imâm)* of the Islamic community—
that is, of all Muslims worldwide—is, according to Shi'i doctrine, the twelfth imam Muhammad al-Mahdî, who was hidden
by his father to protect him from the secular authority, the
Caliph of Baghdad. Since the death of the eleventh imam in
December 873 or January 874, Islam has had no leader present
at all who could rightfully claim succession to the Prophet
Muhammad. The Hidden Imam is said to have still had contact
with his followers until 941 by means of intermediaries, or
"ambassadors," but then he withdrew into the "Greater
Occultation" *(al-ghayba al-kubrâ)*. The institution of "ambassadors" did not prove practicable in the long run and was abandoned. The Shi'a had to develop new models through which to
organize the spiritual leadership of their communities and
establish binding authority. The history of the Shi'a is the history of these attempts, and they continue to this day, as can be
seen by events in Iran.

According to Shi'i theory, the Hidden Imam as successor to
the Prophet and guarantor of the earthly order willed by God is
the only legitimate ruler on earth. Any authority and power
that he did not delegate is regarded presumptuous. Since the
Shi'ites believe that the Hidden Imam did not delegate anyone
to represent him and in his farewell letter even branded as a
fraud anyone who would act in his name in the future, in principle, the Shi'ites consider all forms of rule to be usurpation and
any exercise of power tyranny.

This rigid position evolved from the situation of the Shi'a in
the early Middle Ages. The Abbasid caliphs of Baghdad (749-
1258) were Sunnis. They were considered oppressors of the true
believers and murderers of the martyred imams. The Shi'a was
a minority in the opposition, lacking any prospects of taking
political power, and thus Shi'ites had no difficulty dissociating
themselves from all ruling forces.

Nevertheless, the Shi'a could never have been able to survive if members had not developed community structures and recognized authorities. This was only possible under the condition that all legitimate power was united in the hands of the imam—an extremely difficult undertaking since the imam had not delegated his authority to anyone.

As the sole leader of the community, the imam was theoretically the only one with the right to exercise (or delegate) certain functions. These included all those functions and tasks that the Prophet Muhammad had personally carried out in the original community in Medina. He had led the common ritual prayer *(salât)* of the Muslims and held the sermon *(khutba)*; he led the Muslims in "action" *(jihâd),* that is, in Holy War against the enemies of Islam—the heathen Meccans—and he arbitrated disputes, held court, issued sentences and had them enforced, and he had taxes collected that members of the umma were required to provide for the poor and weaker members of the community. He served simultaneously as leader of a religious and a political community, received and dispatched legates, and he entered into treaties with foreign powers.

When the twelfth imam, the only legitimate successor to the Prophet, disappeared, all of these functions had not suddenly become vacant—as the imam is living somewhere on earth and by no means relinquished his prerogatives—but the exercising of them had been interrupted for an indefinite period of time until his awaited return. Some of the imam's functions were dispensible, as the sect was excluded from political activities anyway. The Shi'ites were never in a position to wage war or run state affairs, nor did they have any judiciary power. But what was the situation in the absence of the imam regarding the ritual duties, especially prayer and the Friday sermon? And what about taxes? Did the requirement to pay taxes to support the poor *(zakât)* or the "fifth" *(khums)* lose its validity until the imam reappeared? And if so, how would the widows and orphans be cared for?

The question of prayer five times daily was the easiest to resolve. Ritual prayer *(salât)* was prescribed in the Quran. It was the individual duty of every Muslim and could be satisfied even without the imam. It was absurd to think that the absence of the imam would release Muslims from this central religious duty. As far as the Friday sermon and the levying of taxes was concerned, however, the problem was much more difficult. Someone had to be entrusted with these tasks, but who should it be and who had the right to do the entrusting?

In formulating such questions, a group of experts in religious and legal affairs emerged: the "scholars" (Arab. al-ulamâ; singular: al-âlim). They are not something particular to the Shi'ites; the Sunnis have the same class of experts with the same name, and the education is very similar, as are the practices. The ulamâ are thus part of Islam as a whole, although among Shi'ites they went through a very specific evolution. Mullâ (mullah) is the Persian word commonly used to address them. It is derived from the Arabic mawlâ, "sir" or "master," a form of address comparable to the Christian "Reverend Father" or the Jewish "Rabbi."

The ulamâ are specialists for religious tradition and law. Originally they were private scholars interested in religious questions, or were collectors, examiners, and commentators of traditional records, that is, statements of the Prophet himself or those of the imams. These traditions were used in formulating instructions for action that applied to one's daily life. The Prophet and his successors, the imams, were considered ideal, perfect Muslims. All reports about them, every word they ever uttered, every action they were observed to have made were considered exemplary and binding. Islamic sciences developed from early collectors' activities and Islamic law is based upon this. Over time, the private scholars became true jurists. The ulamâ do not have the character of priests for either the Sunnis or the Shi'ites. They do not administer any sacraments and they perform the same rituals as all other Muslims. But they are "experts" (Arabic fuqahâ, singular: faqîh) in all areas of knowledge relating to Islam. "Religious scholars" would be an adequate equivalent of the Arabic plural ulamâ.

The Shi'i ulamâ did not only lead the discussion on finding a representative for the Hidden Imam; after centuries of debate and controversy, they gradually assumed one task of the Hidden Imam after another, and the process is still ongoing. The Islamic Revolution in Iran that led the ulamâ, or the mullahs, to take over state power is the preliminary climax to developments that began with the "Greater Occultation," the definitive disappearance of the twelfth imam in the year 941. The following chapter will attempt to provide an overview of these developments and clarify how it was actually possible for the mullahs to lead a revolution and establish a political regime.

2. The Imam's Money: the "Fifth"

The Quran prescribes Muslims to show solidarity with the socially weaker members of the community. A tax called *zakât* serves this purpose (cf. Quran 57:18 and 58:13); the term is normally translated as tax for the poor or "alm tax." The Quran also mentions a tax called "the fifth" *(al-khums)*. (After the death of the Prophet and the establishment of the caliphate, additional taxes were levied, such as the *jizya,* a tax on non-Muslim subjects, and taxes on land used for agricultural purposes. These taxes shall not be considered further here.)

The Quranic *khums* plays an important role for the Shi'ites. According to sura 8:41, "Whatever ye take as spoils of war, lo! a fifth thereof is for God, and for the messenger and for the kinsman (who hath need) and orphans and the needy and the wayfarers." The verb *ghanima* is ambiguous in Arabic. It means both "to achieve or profit" and "to take as spoils." The Sunnis interpret this verse according to the latter definition and apply it only to justify the taxation of war spoils. The Shi'i ulamâ, however, interpret *ghanima* as "to earn" in its broadest sense and since time immemorial have understood the "fifth" as a type of income tax. In principle, every Shi'ite is required to pay one-fifth of all profits—regardless of the trade or business they are from. But to whom? The Quran verse provides the answer, but how is it possible to pay taxes to God or to God's messenger, who has long since died? And who are the kinsmen?

Such questions belong to the domain of the "scholars," the ulamâ. Their method of reasoning and argumentation can be demonstrated using the "fifth" as an example.

The ulamâ take the six categories of potential recipients mentioned in the Quran literally, declaring that each of them is entitled to one-sixth of the fifth. The first three categories—God, the Prophet and his descendents, i.e., the imams—are combined and, accordingly, three-sixths of the *khums* are due the respective imam as the legitimate successor to God's messenger and head of the family of the Prophet. This portion is referred to as the "imam's share" (Arabic *sahm al-imâm;* Persian *sahm-e imâm).* The remaining three categories—orphans, the indigent, and travelers—is not interpreted as needy members of the umma in general, for whom the "poor tax" *(zakât)* is levied, but those orphans, indigent, and needy travelers from the Prophet's family, that is, needy sayyids. Three-sixths of the *khums* are thus allocated to the relations of the Prophet, i.e., all members of the Hâshim clan, to insure that the standard of living of all Hâshimites corresponds to their status. This is the "masters' share" (Arabic *sahm as-sâdât; sâdât* is the Arabic plural of *sayyid).*

But who is responsible for the collection of the *khums* and who distributes it according to divine wishes? And what is done with the "imam's share" as long as the imam remains hidden?

The problem first arose when the original expectation that the Hidden Imam would return quickly proved not to be true. From the early days of the Shi'a, the opinion was passed down that every follower of the faith should save the *khums* at home or even bury it until the imam returned. Others were of the opinion that this tax need not be paid at all as long as the imam remained in hiding. The opinion that finally prevailed among the ulamâ was that the ulamâ themselves were the appropriate trustees to administer the assets of the Hidden Imam. Payment of the *khums* is thus mandatory, even during the absence of the twelfth imam. The ulamâ collect the *khums*, both the "masters' share" and the "imam's share." They distribute the former and use the *sahm al-imâm* they were entrusted with in accordance with the wishes of the Hidden Imam, i.e., for the good of Islam and the umma.

This theory is based on statements by the earliest authority among the Shi'i ulamâ, the Iranian al-Kulaynî, who probably died in Baghdad in 941, the year the "Greater Occultation" began. Around the time of the most significant Shi'i legal scholar of the early Middle Ages, Shaykh Tûsî (died 1067 in an-Najaf), it had already developed to its present form.[1] We must bear in mind that at that time, the Shi'ites were still a minority in the opposition and did not exercise any state authority. Levying and using the *khums* was thus an internal affair of the Shi'i religious community and not an official duty of the state. It has remained that way in principle to this day. By assuming the obligation of distributing one half of the *khums* to the Hâshimites and administering the other half—the Hidden Imam's share—as trustees, the ulamâ have acquired the right of disposal over large sums of money. We shall see that they later gained control of other sources of income in addition to the *khums*. The available funds were channeled mainly into religious, educational, and public welfare institutions. Funds can also be made available for the *jihâd* (as far as this is even possible in the absence of the imam; more on this below); misappropriation is considered a severe transgression against the imam. Many—though not all—mullahs lead an ascetic life; nevertheless, in Iran as in the Christian West there have again and again been complaints and satires about the "greed" of the clergy.

Devout Shi'ites are required to render the *khums* as a voluntary form of self-taxation. There are various ways in which to make the payment. An individual can present the *khums* to any mullah, such as the village mullah. He in turn usually has a type of client relationship to a prominent âyatollâh or grand âyatollâh, to whom he passes on a portion of the collected sum. As a rule the mullah can retain one-third for use by his own village community. The residents of a village or city district or the members of an Âshûrâ guild can also submit the money to an âyatollâh of their choice via a delegate and have a portion of this money returned to them. The amount is usually negotiated with someone authorized by the âyatollâh.[2] Pinault described how the son of the Âyatollâh Khû'i (died 1992), the most highly revered Iraki religious authority, traveled to Hyderabad to collect the *khums* from the observers of the faith. He announced that the âyatollâh had granted permission that a guild there use the entire sum collected for a building program of theirs.[3]

3. Participation in the Government (Tenth to Eleventh Centuries)

As long as the Shi'i communities in Iraq and western Iran remained in the opposition to the Sunni caliphate in Baghdad, it was easy for them to reject all forms of rule and be content to quietly await a speedy return of the Hidden Imam. This situation changed in the tenth century, when they were confronted for the first time with a Shi'i authority. This forced the Shi'i ulamâ to rethink their relationship to state power.

At this time, the Abbasid caliphate was only a shadow of its former self. It was the commanders in chief of the armies, whether Arabic, Turkish, or Iranian, who actually held the power in Baghdad. They challenged each others' rule and appointed or deposed the caliphs as they wished. From 945 to 1055, the office of commander in chief was in the hands of the Bûyids, an Iranian family from the mountainous region south of the Caspian Sea that had always had Shi'i leanings. The Bûyids worked their way up as mercenaries and condottieri and had created outright principalities for themselves in western Iran. In 945 a member of the family also took power in Baghdad. Other branches of the clan ruled in western and central Iran, in Fârs (near Shîrâz), Isfahân, Hamadân, Rey, and Kermân.

Although the Bûyids made no secret of their Shi'i beliefs, they did not challenge the Sunni caliphate. In fact, they needed the caliph to legitimize their own rule. However, they did protect Shi'i communities and approved buildings, presents, and endowments for the shrines of the imams. They assumed the responsibility of protecting the shrines of Karbalâ and an-Najaf, which had been plundered by bedouins several times. In the suburbs of Baghdad, which were predominantly Shi'i, Shi'i festival celebrations were permitted. These included commemoration of the pool of Khumm, where according to Shi'ite tradition Muhammad designated his son-in-law Alî to be his successor, and remembrance of the massacre at Karbalâ (see above, p. 43). Since invectives against the Sunni murderers could commonly be heard at the Âshûrâ processions, there was frequent fighting with Sunnis, who felt provoked by the abusive remarks. It came to rioting in the Shi'i quarter of al-Karkh in 973, and several thousand people died in a major fire. As a result, the government was forced once again to temporarily prohibit the Shi'i processions. In the year 1051, the tombs of the seventh and ninth imams in the northern district, al-Kâzimayn, were even destroyed by Sunnis and the graves of the Bûyid rulers buried there were desecrated.

Under the protection of the Bûyids, the Shi'i communities were able to flourish in Iraq and western Iran, and their sense of identity was strengthened as well, especially since a Shi'i counter-caliphate was established in 909 in present-day Tunisia. The Fatimids, who appeared as successors to the sixth imam, even managed to occupy Egypt in 969 and establish themselves in Cairo, their newly founded residence.[4] Although the Fatimid caliphs were not Twelver Shi'ites, but Ismailis (they were descendents of Ismâ'îl, a son of the sixth imam,

Ja'far), the establishment of a Shi'i caliphate in Egypt served as a powerful impetus for Shi'ism in general. The tenth century could almost be characterized as the "Shi'i century."

Shi'ites enjoyed the favor of the court of the Bûyids of Baghdad and they were enlisted for important tasks. Sharîf at-Tâhir al-Mûsavî, a descendent of the seventh imam, Mûsâ, was repeatedly named the official commander of the Iraqi pilgrim caravans to Mecca. At the same time he served as the representative of the descendents of the Prophet. That is, he was in charge of controlling the lineages and distributing income due the sharîfs from endowments and the *khums*. His sons, Sharîf ar-Radî (died 1015) and Sharîf al-Murtadâ (died 1044), succeeded him in these functions. Ar-Radî even served as deputy to the Sunni caliph regarding judicial appeals to citizen charges of encroachment of their rights by the authorities. The Shi'ites owe to him the extant collection of all speeches, letters, and sermons by Imam Alî. This collection, called "Way of Rhetoric" *(Nahj al-balâgha)* is still respected, even by Sunnis, as a standard work of classical Arabic prose. His brother al-Murtadâ was a highly esteemed Shi'i legal scholar who was frequently present at the court.

Shi'i dignitaries as courtiers of the Abbasid caliphs—who were accused of murdering the imams—what a grotesque situation! No wonder a series of tracts was written titled, approximately, "The Problem of Participating in the Government"; Sharîf al-Murtadâ himself had such an essay written, justifying his own conduct. Alone the fact that he saw a need to issue such a justification serves to show the difficulties involved in a Shi'ite holding political power that was not legitimated through the Hidden Imam.

Precedential cases exist in which a political position was assumed, even under an illegitimate, godless ruler: according to Quran 12:55, the Prophet Joseph did not shy away from commanding even the Pharaoh himself to put Egypt's granary under his charge; and Imam Alî was a member of the council of delegates who elected the hated third caliph Uthmân. Such examples justified al-Murtadâ's participation in the government—under the condition, however, that in carrying out his duties he did not violate any principles of his faith as a Shi'ite. He was required always to act as a secret trustee of the Hidden Imam, protecting and promoting the Shi'a to the best of his ability. An appropriate dictum of the sixth imam Ja'far was of course at hand: "The atonement for participating in the government lies in satisfying the needs of the [Shi'i] brothers." Participating in the government is almost seen as a sacrifice for Shi'ism, even as martyrdom; someone assumes the task of serving a godless tyrant in order to further the cause of true believers.

4. The Foundation of Shi'i Law: the "Four Books"

The era of the Bûyids is the period of the Shi'i "church fathers." The authoritative works of Twelver Shi'i theology and jurisprudence were written in the tenth and eleventh centuries. They were based on sayings of the imams, which correspond to the "sunna" of the Sunnis, that is, the sayings of the Prophet. Since the imams are the legitimate and divine successors of the Prophet, their directives, legal decisions, and instructions for action form a unit with those of the Prophet. Thus the Shi'ites have their own "sunna" (custom, observance, practice, tradition).

The oldest known collection of sayings of the Prophet and the imams that is still in use today is *The Sufficient (al-Kâfî),*[5] a collection supposed to suffice all needs, since it includes *all* sayings of the imams that were known at the time, categorized according to subject area. Volume I deals with creed and imamate; volume II, faith and unbelief; volume III, ritual purity, burial, prayer and zakât (alm tax); volume IV, fasting and pilgrimages, etc. The author of this handbook (eight-volumes in the modern printed edition) was the Iranian al-Kulaynî of Qom, who died in 940 or 941 in Baghdad.

The *Kâfî* is the first of the "Four Books" *(al-kutub al-arba'a)*, on which the entire foundation of Twelver Shi'ism is based. The second of these Four Books is titled *If One Has No Expert at Hand (Man lâ yahduruhu l-faqîh);* in other words, in such a case refer to this book and find everything you need. The author, Ibn Bâbôye al-Qummî (died 991 in Rey, near Tehran), was from Qom (Arabic *Qumm)*, as his epithet reveals, but he taught for a long time in Baghdad. There he left a whole generation of scholars, including the great scholars of the Bûyid epoch, above all the Arab Muhammad al-Hârithî, known by his epithet "the instructing master" *(ash-shaykh al-mufîd)* (died 1022). He taught in a small district mosque in the western part of Baghdad, where he also died. His grave near the shrine of al-Kâzimayn is still visited today. He was the teacher of Sharîf al-Murtadâ (died 1044), mentioned above, who in turn taught al-Tûsî (died 1067), the author of the last two of the "Four Books": *Consideration of the Disputed Traditions* and *Appeal of Decisions.*[6]

Whereas the *Kâfî* by Kulaynî made traditional material available as one of the first collections of sayings by the imams, the four generations of scholars from Qom and Baghdad mentioned above wrote numerous works, developing the principles of jurisprudence *(usûl al-fiqh)*. They were an aid to making decisions for the respective time on the basis of the traditional materials. The aim was not so much to provide solutions for all possible future cases; much more, it was an attempt to secure the principles of the procedure, through which present and future generations of scholars would be in a position, on their own, to answer questions pertaining to any ritualistic, religious, or legal matters.

The Sunnis of course faced the same problem of how to deal with their tradition, the *sunna* of the Prophet. They had already mastered both tasks—the collection of traditional materials and the development of legal principles—earlier than the Shi'ites did. The solutions developed by the Sunnis, however, were only applicable to the Shi'ites to a certain extent. In fact, one of the most important legal principles of the Sunnis was totally unacceptable for the Shi'ites: the "consensus" *(ijmâ')* of Muslims. This term was based on the belief that God would not let all of his community *(umma)* go astray. In other words, if the umma seeks a consensus in essential questions of faith, this is quasi infallible. A traditional saying of the Prophet Muhammad confirms this dogma. For the Shi'ites it was of course unacceptable. As a minority they would always be the losers in such a concept of "consensus." Shi'i legal theory thus only accepts a "consensus" as a legal source if it concurs with the opinion of the infallible imam. A consensus *opposed* to the imam is impossible. For all practical purposes, this eliminated consensus as a legal source.

In place of the Sunni concept of consensus, the Shi'ites use reason *(aql).* Twelver Shi'i religious scholars are rationalists in the sense that even in matters of faith they trust human reason, whereas the Sunnis show greater skepticism toward the capabilities of reason. The basis of Shi'i rationalism is the optimistic conviction that God gave humankind a sense of reason to use in order to recognize God's will. Revelation and reason are by no means mutually exclusive; rather, they are inextricably linked.

The aforementioned scholars of the "Baghdad School" were the first to declare the equal significance of tradition *(naql)* and reason *(aql),* especially Shaykh al-Mufîd and Sharîf al-Murtadâ. However, this principle did not remain undisputed and even later, debate on it continued in Shi'i communities, sometimes causing division. A large majority of âyatollâhs and mullahs today support the rationalist school. They use reasoned argumentation, of which we shall see several examples in the following, and are therefore the exact opposite of "fundamentalists." By using reason and not depending solely on the actual wording of the writings and transmitted sayings of the imams, they secure far wider applicability for their decisions. In addition to this rationalistic cord, which finally predominated to a large extent, there has also always been a "fundamentalist" one, in the original sense of the religious concept. The supporters of this school of thought took—and take—into consideration only the actual wording of the Quranic revelation and the tradition, that is, the sayings of the Prophet and the imams.

5. The New Center: al-Hilla
(Thirteenth to Fourteenth Centuries)

During the period of Bûyid rule (945-1055), Baghdad and Qom were the intellectual centers of the Shi'a. This did not change in the course of the eleventh century, but the Shi'ites did have to adapt to a totally different political situation after the Bûyids were overthrown. This marked the beginning of centuries of central Asian peoples invading and conquering Iran, first the Turks or Turkomans, then the Mongols. Iran was ruled predominantly by nomadic, non-Iranian dynasties until into the twentieth century, from the Turkish Seljuqs in 1038 to the Turkoman Qajars until 1925.

The Seljuqs, a Turkish royal house, led the Turkish nomadic peoples from the steppes around the Aral Sea into Iran. Their leader, Toghril, arranged to be the appointed ruler *(sultân)* in eastern Iran in 1038 and he entered Baghdad in 1055, where he placed the caliph under his "protection" and put an end to Bûyid rule. The Seljuq sultans were zealous Sunnis. Under their rule, the Shi'ites were no longer supported. Shi'i communities in Iraq and the cities of western Iran continued to exist, but they resumed their sectarian, marginal existence.

The situation of the Shi'ites changed dramatically in the thirteenth century. The invasions of the Mongols under the descendants of Genghis Khan brought an end to the Baghdad caliphate. In 1258, Khan Hülägü, grandson of Genghis Khan and brother of the Great Khan Kublai, took Baghdad and had the last Abbasid caliph throttled. The Shi'ites welcomed the end of the hated dynasty. However, their own strongholds were also affected by the Mongol invasion. Qom was destroyed in 1224 and lay in ruins throughout the fourteenth century. Baghdad was reduced to a mere provincial city after 1258; the Shi'i quarter al-Karkh was plundered by the Mongols and the shrine of al-Kâzimayn was destroyed.

A new center of Shi'ism emerged in the small town of al-Hilla on an arm of the Euphrates south of the ruins of Babylon. It developed out of an encampment (Arabic *al-hilla)* of Arab bedouin amirs who had set up a permanent residence. Since the amirs of al-Hilla had been Bûyid vassals, they had adopted the Shi'i faith and brought Shi'i scholars to their small court. When the Mongols arrived, the residents of al-Hilla turned out to be willing collaborators. They built a bridge spanning the Euphrates for the Mongols, thus assuring that the nearby grave of Imam Âli in an-Najaf be spared destruction.

The hopes of the Shi'ites that the new Mongol rulers, who were heathens, would adopt Shi'i Islam were disappointed. Khan Ghâzân became a Sunni in 1295, but the Shi'ites were, nevertheless, once again able to develop more freely under Mongol rule. The small town of al-Hilla became the new center of Shi'i learning, continuing the rationalistic tradition of the "Baghdad School" and once again defining reason as an important principle of jurisprudence. The theoretical foundation laid by the "School of Hilla" in the thirteenth and fourteenth centuries is that upon which the authority of the mullahs and âyatollâhs is based today.

6. The Basis of the Authority of the Mullahs: the Principle of Ijtihâd

The influence of the mullahs on Iranian society and politics has always been puzzling to many western observers. Their taking power came as a surprise to many politicians and journalists. The glittering facade of the shah regime had totally distorted the view of social reality in Iran. In fact, that which suddenly came to the surface was not even all that new.

Iran's Shi'i "clergy"—it will be explained below why this term can be used without hesitation—did not emerge until the sixteenth century, but the foundation of its spiritual power goes back much further, into the Mongol period of the thirteenth and fourteenth centuries.

Only one Shi'i theorist from that time shall be introduced here, the most influential thinker of the al-Hilla school. His true name was al-Hasan ibn Yûsuf ibn Alî ibn al-Mutahhar, though even many Shi'ites do not know him by this name. He is known to all Shi'ites by his honorific epithet *al-Allâma al-Hillî*—"the most learned one of al-Hilla." He was also the first scholar to bear the title *Âyatu'llâh* (sign of God). At that time it was merely an honorary name; only later was it introduced to denote a certain status within a hierarchy.

The Allâma was born in 1250, shortly before the Mongol invasion. He studied in al-Hilla under his father and uncle and later went to Tabrîz in Azerbaijan to the court of the Mongol Khan . . . Öljeitü. He even succeeded in winning the trust of the khan and converting him to Shi'ism. . . . Öljeitü had the names of the twelve imams embossed onto the coins, but this remained an isolated episode; succeeding Mongol rulers of Iran converted back to Sunnism. The Allâma died in 1325 and was buried near the grave of the eighth imam in Mashhad, where he is honored today as a saint.

The most significant theoretical accomplishment of Allâma al-Hillî was the development of the principle of *ijtihâd* legal ruling based on rational considerations. The foundation of the rule of the mullahs in present-day Iran lies in this principle.

The starting point of all theoretical considerations is how to answer questions of a religious, juridical nature if they are not definitively clarified by the Quranic revelation or a saying of an imam (a modern example discussed below is that of birth control). We recall that in Shi'ism, only fourteen persons are considered infallible: the Prophet Muhammad, his daughter Fâtima and the twelve imams. Thirteen of them are dead; one is hidden and thus inaccessible. All other people are subject to error. No one can claim infallibility. What procedure must be taken if a problem cannot be solved by referring to the trans-mitted statements—which are limited? This is where human reason comes in: God gave human beings reason to be used to discover His will. If no answer is offered by tradition *(naql)* then one must gain help from the intellect *(aql)*. A solution so reached, however, like all human decisions, is fallible and there-fore subject to revision at any time.

This rational effort to solve problems is expressed through the Arabic word *ijtihâd,* a verbal noun denoting "making of an effort." The word is related to the familiar term *jihâd* (effort, action), used to denote the struggle for the attainment of God's purposes on earth. The participle of *ijtihâd* is *mujtahid,* trans-lating approximately as "the effort-making one." This is a cen-tral term; the influence of present-day âyatollâhs lies in the fact that they are mujtahids.

Who is a mujtahid? And how does "making an effort," the ijti-hâd, function?

The Allâma al-Hillî wrote a book titled *The Points of Depar-ture from which Knowledge of the Principles is Attained,* which was the first work to provide a theory of ijtihâd.[7] He first described a scholar who has the necessary education, knowl-edge, and capabilities. Most importantly, scholars must totally master the scholarly language, Arabic, in all its subtleties. Knowledge of Arabic is still a basic prerequisite for all theology students at the college in Qom. The Shi'i ulamâ thoughout the world still communicate in Arabic, as occidental scholars were required to have a command of Latin until into the nineteenth century. Mujtahids must also be familiar with the Quranic rev-elation. They are not required to know the entire Quran by heart, as many Muslims do; it suffices if they have a solid foun-dation of about 500 relevant verses. They must also be able to work with the large collections of sayings of the Prophet and the

imams. Of course they must know the principles of jurisprudence and—most importantly—they must have the tools of a
logician, to assure that their decisions are consistent. Ration-
ality and logic are inextricably linked.

This clearly shows that the ability to perform ijtihâd does not
come from inspiration, revelation, or sacramental ordination,
but through scholarship. Becoming a mujtahid involves a long,
intensive course of study. Not everyone is capable of becoming a
mujtahid. The large majority of Shi'ites is excluded from ijtihâd, since "laypeople" are expressly prohibited. The Allâma said
it would even be pernicious if everyone were to start "making an
effort": "if all people were burdened with ijtihâd in legal questions, the world would fall out of joint, for everyone would be
more concerned with the discussion of problems than with earn-
ing their livelihood."[8] In other words, cobblers should stick to
their lasts. The experts should spare them of the difficult and
painful task of ijtihâd.

The ijtihâd is thus reserved for a small number of qualified
specialists, i.e., the mujtahids. One becomes a mujtahid by
being declared one by another mujtahid. To this day this is done
by a teacher granting his pupils the authorization (ijâza) to
exercise ijtihâd on their own.

In contrast to the small, qualified minority of mujtahids,
there are great masses of simple believers in the faith who are
thus relieved of responsiblity for their own decisions. They exercise taqlîd, which approximately means "imitation." A literal
translation of the word is actually "authorization": common
believers authorize the experts to make decisions for them. The
believer who has not studied and is thus not in a position to
made such decisions independently passes to the authority of
an expert. If the mujtahid makes an error in his judgment, the
common believers who entrusted the expert with a judgment
cannot be held responsible.

The mujtahid himself is also permitted to err, since he is not
infallible. It is, however, expected that he make his judgment to
the best of his knowledge and belief; he is accountable for his

decision on Judgment Day. The mujtahids can thus contradict one another, as the Allâma al-Hillî wrote, "sometimes ijtihâd hits the mark and sometimes it does not." To today the following principle applies: "Every mujtahid is right" *(kull mujtahid musîb),* which means that anyone who makes a decision to the best of their knowledge and belief is worthy of obedience. If two mujtahids contradict one another, common believers can choose which opinion to follow; in any case, they are not responsible. The entire system is based on the fallibility of all decisions made in this way. Each individual leader of a religious community can be deemed infallible regarding certain issues, such as has been done by the Catholic Church, but assuming the infallibility of an entire profession would quickly topple the system. Limiting the label of infallible to the "Fourteen"—all of whom are not present and thus cannot be posed any questions—makes up the strength of Twelver Shi'ism; at the same time it is the source of its essential flexibility. All existing authorities are fallible and their judgments can very well be reevaluated and possibly revised by another mujtahid's ijtihâd.

Excluding deceased mujtahids has served to make the system even more flexible. Even Allâma al-Hillî expressed the basic principle as follows: "The deceased have no authority" *(lâ qawla li 'l-mayyit).* An individual Shi'ite cannot challenge the judgment of a living mujtahid by citing the authority of a deceased one. Only living authorities can exercise ijtihâd. There is also a minority opinion that considers the "imitation of the deceased" *(taqlîd al-mayyit)* to be admissible (after Khomeinî's death this question assumed special significance). A living mujtahid can come to the same conclusion on the basis of his own ijtihâd as a deceased colleague but this need not necessarily be the case.

The practice of ijtihâd serves to make Shi'i theology infinitely adaptable and flexible. This does not mean decisions are always made in a progressive and modern sense from a Western perspective. The ijtihâd can lead either to conservative or progressive solutions and it can justify apolitical, quietistic attitudes just as well as revolutionary activism.

The way the ijtihâd functions in practice shall be shown using several examples. As a rule, Shi'ites affiliate themselves with local or regional mujtahids; they form their "communities" and "emulate" them *(taqlîd)*. In addition to the local and regional mujtahids, there are also internationally recognized and respected authorities, the "grand âyatollâhs," whose decisions are followed from Lebanon to India. The formation of a hierarchy will be discussed later.

7. The Emergence of the Shi'i Clergy (Sixteenth Century)

It is problematic to speak of an Islamic "clergy" or "priesthood," since inaccurate associations with Christianity are often made. In Islam—both Sunni and Shi'i—the carriers of religious tradition are not priests, but scholars *(ulamâ)*. They are not ordained, nor do they administer any sacraments. Rather, they have completed a largely legal course of study.

Shi'i mullahs are thus primarily jurists. On the other hand, there are also good reasons to consider them "members of the clergy." In Iran they recently even started referring to themselves as "clergymen" *(rûhâniyyân)*. The development of the Shi'i ulamâ since the Middle Ages to a true clergy, however, was the result of a process that did not begin until the sixteenth century in Iran, culminating in the twentieth century.

In 1501, Ismâ'îl, the youthful leader of a dervish order in Azerbaijan, was able to take power in Iran with the support of nomadic Turkoman tribes. He assumed the Persian title of King of Kings *(shâhân-shâh)* and set up the Safavid dynasty, which ruled Iran until 1722. Ismâ'îl was by no means raised as a strict Twelver Shi'ite and at first he promoted rather unorthodox religious ideas. Soon, however, he recognized the statesmanlike authority of Twelver Shi'ism and declared "Ja'fari" Shi'ism—

named after the sixth imam—to be the state religion of his empire. At this time, only the larger cities of northwestern Iran were Shi'i. Fâtima, Alî, and the other imams were worshipped throughout the country, but Iran was nevertheless still predominantly Sunni. This owed largely to the fact that there were so few educated ulamâ who could have spread Shi'ism. The Safavid shahs, especially Ismâ'îl's successor, Tahmâsp (1524-1576), were therefore dependent on development aid from the Arab countries—southern Iraq, southern Lebanon, and the western (Arabian) coast of the Persian Gulf. The rulers brought a large number of Shi'i ulamâ to these areas to begin setting up a Shi'i infrastructure in Iran. The close family relations of the major mullah families can be traced back to this period. Many Iranian families today still take pride in their Lebanese or Iraqi heritage. Marriage relations beyond the borders are very common, which adds to the solidarity shown by the Shi'i communities in Iran, Iraq, and Lebanon, even in present-day political conflicts.

The most significant scholar in the service of the Safavids was al-Karakî, from the Lebanese Beka'a valley *(al-Biqâ)*. He had lived near the tomb of Imam Alî in an-Najaf since 1504 and answered the call of Shah Ismâ'îl to go to Iran for a period of time. Under Shah Tahmâsp he set up permanent residence in Iran and was showered with honors from the ruling family and endowed with particular authority to spread the Shi'i faith. He was even called the "representative of the (Hidden) Imam."

Karakî's efforts were not undisputed. He supported secular rulers, whose authority was usurped, according to Shi'i dogma, and he granted legitimacy to government actions by issuing legal judgments *(fatwâ)*, an action actually reserved for the Hidden Imam. He installed Shi'i leaders of the Friday prayer *(pîsh-namâz)* throughout the country in the name of the shah and also legitimized the shah's levying of land taxes *(kharâj)*. This tax on the yields of the harvest was supposed to serve the Islamic umma as a whole, according to the ancient Islamic theory, and it was a prerogative of the legitimate leader of the

umma, the imam. Karakî argued that precisely in the interest
of the umma it was not only admissible but even necessary that
a secular—of course Shi'i—leader represent the Hidden Imam
in carrying out this task. He declared that it was not a sin for a
Shi'ite to be paid out of such tax revenue. Karakî based his justification on tracts from the Bûyid period (see above, p. 96),
when similar problems had been dealt with in a similar way.

The politics of the Safavids in spreading Shi'ism throughout
Iran at the same time laid the groundwork to spread clericalism
among the Shi'i ulamâ. This resulted in considerable tension
and conflict between monarchy and clergy. They had worked
hand in hand—each to their own respective advantage—to convert Iran to Shi'ism. The clergy was never a willing tool of the
monarchy. The mullahs were always mistrustful of the abso-
lutist power demands of the monarchy and in 1979 they finally
succeeded in eliminating the monarchy altogether. None of the
Arab or Turkish Sunni countries went through a similar development; in this regard, Iran is unique.

Under the Safavids, a true hierarchy was established in Iran
for the first time. It was headed by a leader (sadr), who did not
so much represent the interests of the "clergy" to the monarch
as to secure state supervision over them. In all major cities of
the empire, regional religious authorities (shaykh al-islâm) and
judges (qâdî) were appointed—in every mosque there was a
prayer leader (pîsh-namâz), in every town with a Friday
mosque there was a leader of the Friday prayer (imâm-jum'a)
and preacher (khatîb). The ruler himself and high-ranking dignitaries increased religious endowments (waqf)—land owner-
ship, urban real estate, commercial firms—whose proceeds
were used to finance religious, charitable, and educational
institutions such as mosques, schools, and colleges or hospitals;
descendents of the Prophet and the imams were (and are) also
maintained. The Shi'i ulamâ were administrators of the already
mentioned "fifth" (khums), especially the "imam's share," as
well as holders of remunerated offices and positions, judicial
experts and notaries, and administrators and direct beneficia-

ries of these endowments, which had grown over centuries to an immense fortune. They therefore had the rights of disposal over a large sum of money—much, much more than their Sunni colleagues had access to. The term "prebend" comes to mind here, which is just what the Greek word "kleros" originally meant.

The most spectacular example of such an endowment is the *waqf* of Shah 'Abbâs I. After taking over Azerbaijan and Georgia in the early 1620s, the shah donated all his private assets—except the crown land—to the "Fourteen Infallible Ones," that is, Muhammad, Fâtima, and the twelve imams. This included land throughout the entire empire, two caravansarais, numerous bath houses *(hammâm)* in various cities, and the four rows of shops *(chahâr bâzâr)* that still mark the four sides of the Shah Square in the new capital of Isfahân. The income from these endowments is certified as inaccessible until the Judgment Day—the Arabic word *waqf* means nothing more than "blocked." It cannot be sold, inherited, or confiscated, and is supposed to benefit the poor, the ulamâ, students of religious law, and all possible religious matters. Such endowments from rulers and other prominent and common Shi'ites throughout the world have added to the endowments of religious institutions, especially the tombs of the imams in an-Najaf, Karbalâ, Baghdad, Sâmarrâ, and Mashhad, as well as the shrine of Qom and many other mausoleums, increasing their value to incalculable proportions.

8. Monarchy and Clergy as Rivals (Seventeenth Century)

The Safavid shahs traced their origin back to the seventh imam, Mûsâ al-Kâzim. Although this could not be verified (and is most likely false), it was commonly believed. The members of the ruling house were considered sayyids or sharîfs, and thus enjoyed the prestige of descendents of the Prophet. The two later Iranian ruling dynasties, the Qajars (1796-1925) and the Pahlavîs (1925-1979) had to do without this religious aura from the outset. But the Safavid shahs, too, who had helped the ulamâ to their esteemed position in Iran in the first place, could by no means rely on their blind obedience. As early as the seventeenth century, as we know especially from reports by European travelers (Jean Chardin 1666; Engelbert Kaempfer 1684-85), there was considerable conflict between the shah and the clergy.

Two claims to power came head to head: On one side the Iranian king of kings, who was part of a two-thousand-year-old monarchic tradition and whose goal was to subject all individual authorities under the absolute rule of the monarchy. On the other side, the clergy, whose legitimacy was based on the claim to represent another absolute, yet hidden sovereignty. The Hidden Imam was thus always a potential challenger to the omnipotence of the king of kings, and the clergy developed into a core of all potential opposition to the absolute monarchy. This is the role it has played in Iran since the seventeenth century,[9] and only from this perspective can one understand the role they played in the 1979 Islamic revolution.

The tension between monarchy and clergy did not exclude the possibility of phases of harmony, even close cooperation. The opposition of individual social groups to the absolutism of the shah did not suffice in and of itself to endanger the monarchy. Not until the interests of the political opposition coincided with those of the ulamâ, uniting the two groups, did it become threatening for the monarch. The threat based on the authority of the Hidden Imam constantly hung over the shah's throne like the sword of Damocles.

Although the Safavid shahs were Shi'ites, their rule was definitely not recognized by all of the Shi'i ulamâ. One of the mullahs of an-Najaf, who had been invited to the courts of Shah Tahmâsp and Abbâs I in the sixteenth century, declined the invitation, remarking that the kingdom of the shah was merely "borrowed." The Iranian monarchs then simply tried to place themselves at the head of the Shi'a. Based on their assumed (and generally acknowledged) descent from the seventh imam, they declared themselves to be the representative of the Hidden Imam, even claiming infallibility *(isma),* a trait traditionally only attributed to the "Fourteen." The Safavids tried to force the ulamâ—like all other individual authorities—under their control. In the conflicts that took place in 1666, as the French traveler Chardin reported, opponents to the tyranny of Shah Abbâs II disguised their opposition in the cloak of religious arguments and agitation. On the outskirts of Isfahân, a mullah named Qâsem—a forerunner of Khomeinî—appeared as a preacher and declared that the shah, who was known to drink wine in public, could not presume to be the representative of God. Only a mujtahid, a qualified scholar, had sufficient knowledge of the religious laws to be in a position to lead believers along the straight and narrow. This was an attempt to counter an "infallible" shah with an "infallible" mujtahid. A candidate was presented as well, namely, the twenty-year-old son of the highest, religious dignitary of Isfahân, the local *shaykh al-islâm.* The pretender was also the son of a Safavid princess, thus combining the attractiveness of being a descendent of the seventh iman with qualified scholarship. The shah arranged that the dangerous mullah disappeared and the opposition silenced.[10] This model of an "infallible mujtahid" did not find general acceptance. It was one of many futile attempts to present a representative of the Hidden Imam. The model of the future was much more one of a *fallible* mujtahid, or to be more exact: the collective of fallible mujtahids, which preserved its dynamic and flexible nature precisely through the principle of fallibility.

The final decades of the Safavid dynasty were marked by renewed close ties between monarchy and clergy. The most significant figure among the mullahs at the end of the seventeenth century was Muhammad Bâqir Majlesî, the shaykh al-islâm who led the coronation ceremony of Shah Husayn I in 1694. He later became a kind of grand inquisitor, and tried to cleanse the

Shi'a in Iran of all heretical remnants of mysticism, philosophy, chiliasm, and gnosis. Majlesî showed no reluctance in seeking advantages from the secular arm of the shah. He considered the exercising of secular power legitimate, not on the basis of any inherent rights of the monarch, but merely as a tool of the mullahs, the collective representation of the Hidden Imam. The shah himself most likely saw it differently, but as long as each side found some advantage in the cooperation, the basic incompatibility of their points of view remained veiled.

Majlesî tried another time to collect all the sayings of the Prophet and the imams. His comprehensive work, the *Seas of Lights (Bihâr al-anwâr),* comprised 110 volumes in modern print. When he died in 1700, he was interred at the Friday mosque of Isfahân, where he is still honored today as a saint. His shrine has become a local pilgrimage site.

9. Rationalists and Traditionalists (Seventeenth and Eighteenth Centuries)

The Shi'i theology that was spread by the Iraqi and Lebanese scholars brought to Iran by the Safavids was that of the "School of Hilla." The doctrine of the Allâma al-Hillî deals with the responsible role of the expert capable of ijtihâd, the process of logical judgment. The name of the school of Shi'i rationalists, the Usûlî School, is derived from the practice of reasoning based on prescribed binding principles (Arabic *usûl).*

The school's doctrine did not remain uncontested. Not only Sunnis, but some Shi'i theologians as well, were skeptical of what human reason was capable of and wanted to leave it out of the discussion of issues of divine revelation totally. For them, the only acceptable sources aside from the text of the Quranic revelation were sayings and actions of the Prophet and the imams that were confirmed by ear and eyewitnesses. The theoretical foundation of this traditionalistic school, called the

Akhbârî School after the traditional reports (Arabic *akhbâr)* recognized by them as the sole source of truth, was developed by a mullah named Muhammad Amîn Astarâbâdî (died 1624). He contested the ulamâ's ability to make legal judgments through ijtihâd, thus questioning their collective representation of the Hidden Imam. The Akhbârîs challenge the monopolistic position of the mujtahids and their claim to be emulated *(taqlîd)* by followers of the faith. They see all followers as having a right to draw from traditional sources directly and without mediation.

The Akhbarîs are the Shi'i "fundamentalists" in the true sense of the word. Unreflected use of the word "fundamentalism" by the media to denote all sorts of militant and revolutionary groups and movements in the Islamic world has emptied the term of any precise meaning, so that it has become nothing more than a meaningless label. On top of that, the term, originally associated with the scholarly study of religions, is totally inappropriate in refering to modern forms of political Islam. It is not possible simply to transfer terminology from the field of religious studies to a political sphere. This can be clearly demonstrated in the area of Shi'ism. It is generally assumed that Shi'i revolutionaries are Iran's "fundamentalists." The vague idea behind this characterization is most likely that the establishment of a legitimate Islamic state and social order is in itself "fundamentalist." Fundamentalism in its original and strict sense, however, is something else. It is the limitation of binding truth to the strict wording of the revelation or tradition and the acceptance of nothing else. Pietistic Protestants, Catholic "Creationists," and Jehovah's Witnesses, all of whom take the text of the Biblical story of Creation literally and oppose the scientific explanation of evolution, are fundamentalists. The Shi'i Akhbârîs, who reject ijtihâd, are also fundamentalists. The Usûlîs, however, advocates of ijtihâd, the practice of responsible reasoning and drawing conclusions, are the exact opposite of fundamentalists.

The Akhbârî School, which competed with the Usûlî School

during the eighteenth century for the favor of the Iranian monarch, lost in the end and became a marginal group. Today, most Akhbârî supporters live outside Iran, in the Iraqi city of Basra or in Bahrain. The victory of the Usûlî School was not won in Iran, but in Iraq, especially in an-Najaf.

The graves of the imams in Iraq—in an-Najaf, Karbalâ, al-Kâzimayn near Baghdad, and Sâmarrâ—play a special role in the history of modern Shi'ism, in particular because they lie outside of the largely Shi'i Iran. We have already spoken of the tension-filled relationship between the monarchy and the clergy in Iran. Whenever Shi'i ulamâ came into direct conflict with the shah, they could seek refuge on the "thresholds" *(al-atabât)* of the holy imams and were thus protected from the shah's grasp, especially since 1638, when Iraq became a province in the Turkish Ottoman Empire. The Sunni Ottomans were occasionally welcomed by the Iranian opposition, since they actively pursued politics and propaganda against the shah. When Khomeinî was sent into exile from Iran by the shah, he settled in 1965 in an-Najaf to organize the revolution from there. With that, he was continuing a tested, two-hundred-year-old model.

The Iraqi Shi'ites were generally left alone by the Ottomans. In the eighteenth century, the shrines at Karbalâ and an-Najaf even started surpassing the Iranian centers of Shi'ism, especially since Iran remained without a strong central authority for the rest of the century after the Safavid dynasty ended in 1722. First there was foreign rule by the Sunni Afghans, and then it broke down into regional dynasties and was ruled by Turkoman tribal lords. During the short period of rule by Nâdir Shâh (1736-1747), Iran was even supposed to be converted back to Sunnism. At that time, numerous prominent Iranian ulamâ fled Nâdir's tyranny to Iraq to settle at the shrines.

The leading figure of the ulamâ of Karbalâ at this time was Muhammad Bâqir Vâhid Behbihânî (1705-1790) of Isfahân, who stayed in Karbalâ after completing his studies there. He spoke out for the interests of the Usûlî School and pushed through the concept of ijtihâd. He openly attacked his Shi'i adversaries by declaring any and all opponents of ijtihâd to be unbelievers *(kâfir)* and having his armed guards, the "masters of wrath," intimidate them. "Declaring someone to be an unbeliever" *(takfîr)* became a practicable weapon of the mujtahids in their struggle for the Usûlî doctrine and against all divergent scholarly opinions. In this way, Twelver Shi'ism, especially in the nineteenth century, was rigorously cleansed of all competing, older traditions (mysticism, gnosis, chiliasm) as well as "heretical" innovations such as Shaykhism, Bâbism, Bahâ'ism. Vâhid Behbihânî is considered the "renewer" *(mujaddid)*, even the true "founder" *(mu'assis),* of orthodox Shi'ism as it would also become accepted in nineteenth century Iran.

10. Secular and Spiritual Arm (Nineteenth Century)

A confederation of northern Iranian Turkoman nomadic tribes came out of the chaos of the eighteenth centruy as victors. They were the Qajars and their leader took on the title "king of kings" *(shâhân-shâh)* in 1796. The residence of the Qajar ruling house in Tehran, at the foot of the Elburs mountains, became the new capital of Iran.

The Qajar shahs, who ruled in Iran until 1925, had no religious legitimacy whatsoever. The title "king of kings" was part of the ancient, pre-Islamic tradition of the Iranian kingdom. In order to stabilize their rule, it was absolutely necessary secure their position with respect to the Shi'i clergy, as all opposition could have otherwise easily made use of religious arguments. The first two Qajar shahs thus claimed to be devout Shi'ites; the founder of the dynasty had the remains of his ancestors from Astarâbâd (southeast of the Caspian Sea) brought to the shrine of an-Najaf and had the dome on the shrine of Karbalâ gilded. The second ruler, Fath 'Alî Shâh (1797-1834), took a pilgrimage every year from Tehran to Qom to the tomb of Fâtima-ye

Ma'sûme. He also freed the residents of the city of all taxes, and had the Feyziyya, the theology law college *(madrasa)* next to the tomb and the Friday mosque, renovated. The Feyziyya became the center of the Islamic revolution in 1963 and is presently the spiritual and intellectual center of Iranian Shi'ism.

The shrine of Karbalâ fell victim to a radical anti-Shi'i Sunni reaction in 1802. Towards the end of the eighteenth century the puritanical renewal movement of the Wahhâbites emerged on the Arabian peninsula. The movement founder, Preacher Muhammad ibn Abd al-Wahhâb (1703-1792), was supported by the military strength of the Sa'ûd clan, who thereby gained access to the royal house. The Wahhâbites, "fundamentalists" in the original, scholarly sense of the word, reject as heretical "innovations" *(bid'a)* all religious practices not explicitly permitted according to the actual wording of the Quran and the Sunna. This includes what they consider the un-Islamic worship of saints and the related visits *(ziyâra)* to gravesites. The Shi'i cult of the imams is sheer idolatry, according to the Wahhâbites. They consider splendidly ornamented shrines to be quasi heathen temples. During an attack of the wealthy pilgrimage site at Karbalâ in April 1802, pious zeal joined forces with eagerness for the booty and the Wahhâbites destroyed the shrine of Prince of the Martyrs al-Husayn, killing approximately 2000 people. In 1803 they conquered Mecca, followed by Medina in 1805. Here, too, they desecrated all sacred sites and tombs. At the Baqî' cemetery in Medina, they destroyed the shrines of four imams, al-Hasan, Alî Zayn al-Âbidîn, Muhammad al-Bâqir, and Ja'far as-Sâdiq. To this day the incompatibility of Wahhâbism and Twelver Shi'ism has intensified the—politically motivated—rivalry between the Kingdom of Sa'ûdî Arabia and the Islamic Republic of Iran for predominance in the Gulf region.

As Turkomans, the Qajar shahs could lay no claim to any religious authority. They were prevented at the outset from inventing a story of descent from one of the imams—as the Safavids had succeeded in doing. They were thus dependent on the cooperation of influential Shi'i ulamâ and tried to the best of their ability to support the ulamâ and bring them to their court. The ulamâ were open to working together with the dynasty to a limited extent, but their deeply rooted mistrust of the monarchy remained. More than a few ulamâ refused to go to Tehran and "besmirch" themselves with the monarchy. In addition, there were still religious movements in Iran that were a thorn in the side of the Usûlî School ulamâ. The third Qajar shah, Muhammad Shâh (1834-1848), showed a leaning toward mysticism and supported the dervish orders through large endowments. As a result, some of the ulamâ immediately sided with the opposition to the crown and supported rebel princes.

Since the kingdom of the Qajars had no religious legitimacy, it was tolerated by the ulamâ only as long as their interests coincided. This was the case until the mid-nineteenth century. There was a sort of "unspoken agreement" and throughout the Qajar dynasty, the ulamâ circulated no tracts pronouncing the illegitimacy of secular rulers.[11] The doctrine followed was reminiscent of that of the "two swords," through which medieval state theorists attempted to grasp the relationship between emperor and pope. Both authorities were given a task by God, and these complementary tasks served the same goal of maintaining the divine order on earth. Sayyid Ja'far Kashfî (died 1850) formulated the theory as follows: Representation of the Hidden Imam—who alone unites the spiritual *and* secular leadership in his person—is divided during his occultation. The secular arm of the monarch is responsible for law and order and protection of the country militarily, whereas the ulamâ have the role of the spiritual guardian. They confirm the legitimacy of all government actions and monitor the maintenance of the revealed, divine order *(sharî'a)*.

The example of the jihâd can be used to illustrate how this worked in practice. The struggle for the Islamic cause, the "action"—this is the most precise translation of the Arabic word—is one of the most important tasks of the imam as head of the umma. During the imam's absence the shah must assume this task. If he neglects to perform it properly, the ulamâ make reminders or even take the matter into their own hands. In the early nineteenth century the Russians started expanding into the countries south of the Caucasus Mountains that had been conquered by Iran at the end of the sixteenth century, i.e., Georgia, Armenia, and Azerbaijan. When the Iranian defense failed, Fath 'Alî Shâh was put under pressure. It was feared that the Muslim peoples of the Causasus would come under the rule of unbelievers—a classic situation calling for jihâd. In 1809 one of the most significant contemporary Shi'i scholars, Shaykh Ja'far Kâshif al-Ghitâ, took the view that during the occultation of the Hidden Imam, the scholars have not only the right but the obligation to exercise ijtihâd to determine if jihâd is justified; if so, he wrote, they must declare it. Kâshif al-Ghitâ felt justified in making such a decision in his role as mujtahid, or qualified scholar. He demanded not only that the inactive shah prepare for jihâd against the Russians, but also that the "imam's share" *(sahm-e imâm)*, i.e., half of the *khums* paid by the believers of the faith, should be made available to this end. The shah finally submitted to the pressure of the ulamâ, the results of which were devastating. In the second war with Russia, Iran lost the three provinces south of the Caucasus; they were ceded to Tsarist Russia in 1828 in the peace treaty of Turkumânchây.

11. Marja' at-taqlîd: the Source of Imitation

During the nineteenth century the School of the Usûlîs— "supporters of the principles"—i.e., advocates of independent legal decisions based on rational considerations *(ijtihâd),* was finally able to gain widespread acceptance over all other inner-Shi'i schools of thought, in both Iraq and Iran. The fundamentalist "traditionalists" (Akhbârî) became an insignificant group on the periphery. Armed with the weapon of *takfîr* ("declaring to be unbelieving"), the mujtahids tried to cleanse the Shi'a of all remnants of mystical, gnostic, or chiliastic religious forms, and forced newer religious movements such as Shaykhism, Bâbism, and Bahâ'ism out of the narrowed circle of orthodoxy. During this time Twelver Shi'ism evolved into its present form. The theory that all the tasks of the Hidden Imam should be assumed in his absence by qualified scholars had thus found ultimate acceptance. A summary of these tasks was prepared as early as the tenth century by al-Kulaynî, the earliest collector of sayings of the imams: "The imam is in charge of leading prayer, levying alm taxes, organizing periods of fasting [during Ramadân], the pilgrimages *(hajj)*, jihâd, budgeting of community property *(fay)* and alms, enforcing corporal punishment [as prescribed in the Quran] *(hudûd),* making legal judgments, and defending the borders."[12]

All these responsibilities were now transferred to the qualified scholars, or mujtahids. According to their own interpretation they could make use of the secular arm in completing these tasks. Authorization to perform ijtihâd, that is, using reasoning to make decisions, is reserved for only very few scholars. Ideally, as explained in 1809 by Kâshif al-Ghitâ, the final decision is made by the best (Arabic *al-afdal)* or the most knowledgeable *(al-a'lam)* of the scholars. But who is the best and most knowledgeable? What demands are made of him and—most importantly—how is it determined who he is? These questions have continued to occupy mujtahids to today. There has been a noticeable trend toward the establishment of a hierarchy. Although theoretically all qualified scholars collectively represent the Hidden Imam, the postulate of a top level of authority has evidently answered a deep-seated need. Fallible, mutually contradicting mujtahids and the provisional nature of their decisions might be acceptable in theory, but a desire for a highest, generally recognized authority had come up again and again.

The position of the "best scholar" was not institutionalized in Iran prior to the Islamic revolution. Nevertheless, since the

nineteenth century there have been individual, prominent mujtahids who were granted the status of being generally recognized authorities on account of their abilities and popularity.
They were made "sources of imitation" *(marja' at-taqlîd)*, i.e.,
their example was widely considered binding and their opinions
were generally sought and accepted, far beyond the local or
regional sphere over which a mujtahid commonly had jurisdic-
tion. We recall that *taqlîd*—approximately "imitation, subjec-
tion to an authority"—is the complement to *ijtihâd* (independent legal judgment). Whereas only few experts were qualified
and authorized to exercise ijtihâd, the common masses of
believers were supposed to practice *taqlîd*, i.e., to bow to a higher authority and be guided by it.

The qualities required of the "best" and "most knowledgeable" scholar and the criteria for recognizing them are still disputed, even among mujtahids themselves. There are countless
controversies revolving around the question of the "highest
qualification" *(a'lamiyya)*. Some Shi'ites almost doubt that
there could even be such a single person who unites all imagin-
able requirements. They support the idea of cooperative forces
and the creation of a collective *a'lamiyya* by appointing a council of the highest mujtahids. In practice the *marja's* have always
been determined without any formal procedure. Their status
has derived of spontaneous recognition by the believers of the
faith.

The first mujtahid recognized by all Twelver Shi'ites as
marja' at-taqlîd was Mortazâ Ansârî (died 1864) from
Khûzistân (southwestern Iran). He lived and worked for an
extended period of time in Iran, moving to an-Najaf in 1833.
The Iraqi shrines remained the spiritual centers of Shi'ism
throughout the nineteenth century. Not until the twentieth century were they superceded by Qom.

Ansârî did not have any direct successor. A considerable period of time passed until Mîrzâ Muhammad Hasan Shîrâzî was
generally accepted as a new marja'. He settled at the shrine of
the tenth and eleventh imams in Sâmarrâ and will be discussed

below in connection with the conflict surrounding the tobacco monopoly. After his death as well, there was no generally recognized highest authority for a long time. In the 1920s there were three rivalling marja's who shared the honor, two of whom also resided at an-Najaf in Iraq (Isfahânî and Nâ'înî), and a third, Âyatollâh Hâ'erî (died 1937), who helped Qom assume a leading role in Shi'i spiritual life and was Khomeinî's spiritual master.

Starting in 1949, a third undisputed mujtahid was generally recognized as the highest marja'. This was Âyatollâh Husayn Borûjerdî, who taught in Qom. When he died in 1962, Shah Muhammad Rezâ Pahlavî tried in vain to give the honor of the highest marja' to a non-Iranian in order to stem the influence of the clergy in his country. The shah sent a telegram with the news of the death of Borûjerdî to the Iraqi âyatollâh al-Hakîm in an-Najaf and attempted to designate him as successor. But the Shi'a in Qom had meanwhile become strong enough to reject the pre-eminence of an-Najaf and no longer tolerated an Arab as the highest marja'.

Since 1962 there have been at least eight scholars who have exercised the highest spiritual authority and were widely recognized as marja' at-taqlîd. There were three in an-Najaf: the Arab al-Hakîm and the Iranians Shâhrûdî and Khû'î; one in Tehran (Khwânsârî), one in Mashhad (Mîlânî), and three in Qom (Golpâyegânî, Mar'ashî, and Sharî'at-Madârî).[13] The pre-revolutionary events of 1963-64 led to the expulsion of Khomeinî. He had been unknown until then but had entered the spotlight for the first time and became spokesman for the clerical opposition to the shah regime by settling in 1965 at the shrine of an-Najaf. He quickly rose to the status of marja'. When Khomeinî constitutionally attained the status of "leader" *(rahbar)* of the revolution in 1979, it brought totally new—and not undisputed—elements into the traditional, informal hierarchy of the Shi'i clergy. The attitudes of the other marja's fluctuated from agreement to clear restraint (Khû'î, Golpâyegânî, Mîlânî, Khwânsârî) to open opposition (Sharî'at-Madârî) regarding the role of the "leader."

After the revolution, in the early 1980s, there were eight muj-tahids in addition to Leader of the Revolution Khomeinî who were recognized as marja' at-taqlîd. Only one resided in Iraq (Khû'î) and seven in Iran: Sharî'at-Madârî, Mar'ashî, and Golpâyegânî in Qom, Shîrazî and Qommî in Mashhad, Khwânsârî in Tehran, Mahallâtî in Shîraz.

The number of marja's has since declined. Sharî'at-Madârî died in 1986 after spending the final years of his life under house arrest. Khomeinî died in 1989; the learned book collector Mar'ashî died in 1991, and Âyatollâh Khû'î, at 93 years of age, in 1992 in an-Najaf. Khû'î enjoyed the greatest authority of all marja's; even the Shi'ites in Hyderabad, India, recognized him as their "source of imitation" and paid their khums to him. Saddam Hussein had tried in vain to exploit Khû'î for his polit-ical goals. After the deaths of the 95-year-old Âyatollâh Golpâyegânî (1993) and the 102-year-old Âyatollâh Arâkî (1994), there was an open conflict over a successor generally recognized as the highest marja'. Promising candidates were Âyatollâh Mohammad Rûhânî, who taught in Qom and whose followers live primarily in Pakistan and East Africa, and Âyatollâh Sîstânî, a teacher in an-Najaf who could mobilize supporters in the Arab countries and on the Indian subconti-nent, but hardly in Iran. The revolutionary regime in Iran tried directly following Arâkî's death in December 1994 to have Khâmene'î, Khomeinî's successor as the leader (rahbar) of the Iranian revolution, recognized as the single marja' at-taqlîd of all Shi'ites. A number of prominent Friday preachers and some organizations of the revolutionary clergy made public state-ments supporting Khâmene'î. But according to opinions at the time, Khâmene'î was much too young for this position and was not yet recognized as a theological authority, so that Khâmene'î himself soon renounced his claim. He declared that he by no means regarded himself as the highest marja', since there were a number of other candidates equally worthy of the position.

The marja's have been given the highest status in the now

common, inflated hierarchy of titles as the Grand Âyatollâh *(Âyatu'llâh al-uzmâ)*. The concentration of spiritual authority on a—variable—number of very few "sources of imitation" has not changed the fundamental assumption of the fallibility of the mujtahids. No marja' is considered infallible and every decision is provisional and can be revised—through the ijtihâd of another marja'. In practice, of course, the authority of the "sources of imitation" should not be discredited by frequent recantation, as that would be detrimental to the reputation of the entire class of scholars.

12. The Struggle against Westernization

The social influence of the Iranian mullahs in the nineteenth century owed primarily to the double role they assumed— admittedly in their own interest. On the one hand, they represented interests of the public to the foreign (Turkoman) ruling house of the Qajars; on the other hand they saw themselves as the guarantors of Iranian interests in the face of the increasing, especially economic European influence in Iran. They continue to play this popular, "national" role to this day and the revolution of 1979 cannot be understood without taking this aspect of their activities into account.

With respect to both of these roles, the Shi'i clergy is closely tied to the *bâzâr*, to traditional business in Iranian cities, to handcrafts, trade, and moneylending. The mullahs' social ties to the mostly middle-class businesspeople are not only due to their own background, relatives, and relations by marriage, but because they receive their livelihood from this group of people. The "fifth" *(khums)*, including the "imam's share," which is administered by the mullahs, is collected largely from the income of the businesspeople at the bazaar. Since all Shi'ites can decide on their own which mujtahid they pay their tithes to, the bâzârîs have an instrument of control at their disposal.

They can support individual mujtahids with their loyalty and their money, letting others "hunger"; mujtahids who are not in a position to make charitable donations, such as covering the modest cost of living of their students, quickly lose influence.

The joint interest group of bazaar and clergy was largely responsible for the success of the 1979 revolution. It had already repeatedly proven effective in the nineteenth century. Around 1850, the Qajar shahs—like the Ottoman sultans in Istanbul—initiated a series of reforms aimed at turning Iran into a modern state in a European sense. Nâsiroddîn Shâh (1848-1896) brought European advisors into the country in the areas of military, justice, and education, and not only that: He brought in European capital and European entrepreneurs as well, who—for the benefit of both sides—established themselves in Iran and took control of significant branches of the Iranian economy. Traditional Iranian businesspeople—i.e., "the bazaar"—felt threatened by these developments. If the bâzârîs became impoverished, then the flow of *khums* could dry up. Moreover, through the establishment of modern educational facilities and new, judicial structures modelled after European systems, the Shi'i clergy had lost two spheres of activity that they had monopolized since time immemorial.

It is beyond the scope of this book to describe in detail the tension-filled and moving developments in the relationship between monarchy and clergy in the nineteenth century. One case shall be mentioned, however, as it implemented methods characteristic of those used by the mullahs to gain influence. It is the well-known conflict over the tobacco concession.

In promoting the Iranian economy (and his own income), the shah granted foreign states and companies a number of privileges and monopolies. The Russians, for example, received fisheries rights for all of the Caspian Sea in 1879, and in 1889, the British were allowed to found the *Imperial Bank of Persia*. The selling out of domestic economic interests reached its peak when the shah transferred the concession for all marketing of Iranian tobacco production for fifty years to a British company, the *Imperial Tobacco Company*. In return, the shah received an annual fixed payment of 15,000 pounds sterling and a fourth of the profits. Local tobacco growers were not hurt much by the deal; the monopoly even secured them a regular income. The economic interests of the wholesalers and traditional money-lenders of the bazaar, however, were greatly affected. When they revolted, the mullahs were ready and willing to lend them the spiritual sword for the battle against the "unbelievers." Riots broke out in the summer of 1891 in Tabrîz, in northern Iran. Not only were the shops of the bazaar closed—which has always been a storm warning in the orient—but the religious colleges, or madrasas, closed their doors as well. There was no more obvious way for bâzârîs and mullahs to demonstrate that they stood side by side. Shîrâzî (see above, p. 120), generally recognized at the time as the highest marja', sent a protest telegram to the shah from his Iraqi residence at the shrine of Sâmarrâ. A legal decision *(fatwâ)* that was circulated in Tehran in December 1891 proved to be much more effective, however. There were rumors that it was issued by Shîrâzî (which to this day has not been confirmed). It declared all tobacco consumption to be an act of aggression "against the present imam [i.e. the hidden, Twelfth Imam]—may God speed his return!" With the help of both bâzârîs and mullahs, the fatwâ spread like wildfire throughout Iran. In no time, pipes and waterpipes disappeared from the coffee houses; smoking was abandoned in all of Iran. The British company felt swindled and demanded that the shah take back the concession, which had since become useless. The shah complied in January 1892 and in the same month a new fatwâ was transmitted by telegram that lifted the controls on smoking. This fatwâ is confirmed to have come from Marja' Shîrâzî in Sâmarrâ.

In the conflict over the introduction of a constitution in 1906, many Iranian mullahs stood at the side of the liberal constitutionalists, but this was not because they had taken up the cause of the democratization of the country; rather, they viewed any weakening of the absolute monarchy as a strengthening of their own position. Most mullahs were in fact mistrustful of the constitutional movement. They sought to reinforce their own influence by pushing through Article 2 of an amendment to the constitution of October 7, 1907. This amendment subjected all decisions of the parliament to the control of a council of five mujtahids. The council had the task of verifying whether a law was compatible with the divine system of law of the sharî'a. The clergy thus secured the right of veto for all decisions of the legislative assembly. Since the constitution became virtually ineffective after the shah dissolved the second parliament in 1911, this famous Article 2 became obsolete. It was never forgotten, however, and was again referred to during the drafting of the constitution of the Islamic Republic in 1979.

After the Qajar dynasty was toppled and power was taken by former military leader Rezâ Khân, under the royal name "Rezâ Shâh Pahlavî", the Iranian clergy was forced into the defensive. Rezâ Shâh (1925-1941) was an admirer of Kemal Atatürk; he tried, like Atatürk, to convert his country into a modern laical state. All particular powers—provincial rulers, aristocracy, nomadic princes, clergy—were forced under the autocratic rule of the monarch. Attempts were made to break the social influence of the mullahs. As Atatürk had done, Rezâ Shâh made it compulsory for men to wear European clothing (1929) and prohibited women from wearing a veil, or *châdor* (1936). By allowing only mullahs and theology students *(talaba,* pl. *tullâb)* to wear the traditional caftan and turban, and by establishing a state examination commission to pronounce their recognition as clergy, the shah actually completed the process of clericalizing the ulamâ. From this point on, the ulamâ were defined as having special status and were identifiable through their dress. Public displays of mourning during the month of Muharram were halted and flagellation and passion plays prohibited. School curriculum and the legal system were secularized. Study of law and theology were transferred to the Tehran University, founded in 1935, which thus placed them under state control. Only students who studied law there were permitted to become

judges. The mullahs' activities were limited to religious matters; in 1932 they lost their monopoly on certification and docu-
mentation of legal transactions—a kind of notarial function,
especially in rural areas—and with it they lost one of their most
lucrative sources of income. A large segment of college students
allowed themselves to become swept up in the call of the modern age. The young generation of intellectuals had liberal, secular, and anti-clerical attitudes.

When Rezâ Shâh's efforts to follow the German Empire
caused the Allied powers to force him to abdicate to his son
Muhammad Rezâ, repression of the clergy decreased considerably. The weakness of the young shah was exploited by the clergy to win back some of their lost ground. In 1948, fifteen leading mujtahids issued a fatwâ declaring that wearing the châdor
was compulsory and the shah did not dare oppose them. The
Âshûrâ customs, including processions of flagellants and
ta'ziyeh performances, which had been repressed by Rezâ Shâh,
experienced a revival. But the new shah was unwavering in
retaining the laical course of his father, especially once he
returned to the throne with the support of the United States
after the nationalist interlude of Prime Minister Mosaddeq
(1951-53). In the ten years from 1953 to 1963, ancient tensions
between monarchy and clergy—which went virtually unnoticed
in the West—once again intensified until finally breaking out in
all severity.

13. The Rise of Qom

Qom, a city lying 140 kilometers southwest of Tehran, is one
of the oldest centers of Shi'ism on Iranian soil. Its leading role
as a stronghold of the Islamic revolution, however, is very
recent.

The old Iranian city of Qom was most likely destroyed during
the Arab-Islamic invasion of Iran in the middle of the seventh

century. It had already been resettled in 712 or 713 by Shi'i
Arabs from Kufa and retained its character as an Arab colony
for several centuries. In 816 or 817, Fâtima "the Infallible"
(al-Ma'sûma), sister of the eighth imam, died here and the city
owes its appeal to her grave. In the tenth century, Qom and
Baghdad were the most important centers of Twelver Shi'i
intellectual life. Several significant authors from this time had
the (Arabic) name al-Qummî, denoting their origin. In 1224 the
city was destroyed during the first Mongol invasion and it lost
all importance for centuries. Not until the fourteenth century
did it regain significance, when the Shi'i dynasty of the Safavids
(1501-1722) brought Qom back to life. Before Iraq came under
the rule of the Sunni Ottomans in 1638, Shah Abbâs I (1588-
1629), in particular, tried to lure Shi'i pilgrims from the imam
gravesites in Iraq to the two Iranian shrines at Mashhad and
Qom. He made rich endowments to the shrine of Fâtima-ye
Ma'sûme and had a school and a pilgrim hospice built there.
Many of his successors had themselves interred in Qom. The
theological law school (madrasa) in Qom was founded very
early, in 1533; it is commonly known as the Feyziyya (Arabic
after the famous religious scholar, Muhsin Feyz (Arabic Fayd)
Kâshânî, who taught there.

Qom's proximity to Tehran, which became the royal residence
under the Qajars (1796-1925), proved beneficial for the city. The
tomb with the gilded dome, the Friday mosque next to it with a
large, tiled dome, and the directly adjacent madrasa, the
Feyziyya, were given their present form through endowments of
the Qajar shahs, who chose Qom as their preferred place of burial.

The Feyziyya was renovated in 1798 by the Qajar Fath 'Alî
Shâh. It has a rectangular courtyard, surrounded on all four
sides by two-story wings that open onto the courtyard with
domed alcoves. Student residences are in the wings and in the
middle of each wing is a large, domed hall (aiwân) that opens
entirely onto the courtyard, which is used for instruction. The
professor lectures here encircled by students sitting on the
ground.

During the nineteenth century, the Feyziyya of Qom could not compete with the other intellectual centers of Shi'ism. The Iraqi shrines or "thresholds" *(atabât)*, especially an-Najaf, enjoyed much greater prestige. That did not change until the 1920s. Qom's rise owes to the Âyatollâh Abd al-Karîm Hâ'erî Yazdî (1859-1937). After completing studies at the shrines in an-Najaf and Sâmarrâ, Hâ'erî, a scholar from Yazd in central Iran, had settled in the western Iranian city of Arâk and then moved to an-Najaf and Karbalâ, finally returning to Arâk in 1913. Such changes of residence for studying and training purposes is very common among the Shi'i ulamâ. In 1922 he was invited to Qom, where he then settled and started reforming the archaic teaching structures at the Feyziyya. The madrasa had slightly more than 1000 theology students *(talaba)* at that time. Hâ'erî drew a large number of his students—including Khomeinî—to the sleepy city of Qom. Numerous Iranian ulamâ followed shortly thereafter. They had been studying or teaching at the "thresholds" in Iraq and were forced to leave the country for expressing their disapproval of the "alliance treaty" between Great Britain and Iraq. King Faisal of Iraq had signed the treaty in 1922, subjecting Iraq to Great Britain's imperial interests. Qom became the meeting place for an anti-imperialist elite of younger, religious, yet also politically involved intellectuals. This elite, along with their students, would provide the revolution with definitive momentum.

Âyatollâh Hâ'erî is the true founder of the theological "research center" *(howza-ye elmiyye,* Arabic *al-hawza al-ilmiyya)* in Qom. The Arabic word *hawza* literally means "property, district, territory"; it corresponds approximately to the word *campus* of the Anglo-American university system. The hawza has long since grown beyond the walls of the old Feyziyya School and now includes numerous building complexes throughout the city. The original Feyziyya building was extended after the revolution. A second courtyard with four residential wings was added. On the outskirts of the city a totally new madrasa named after the local saint Fâtima-ye Ma'sûme and a college for women were built. The hawza now includes about 100 institutes. The number of students increased rapidly after the revolution. During Hâ'erî's time there were about 1000 students, at the time of the revolution in 1979 there were about 6000, and as of 1993 there are 25,000 students, 3000 of whom are foreign students from throughout the Islamic world. Approximately 1000 students are women. The administration of the hawza is presently planning to increase residential and teaching capacities to accommodate 100,000 students in the future. Whether or not this dream will ever be fulfilled remains to be seen. During the Iran-Iraq war in 1980-88, 2500 students from Qom who volunteered to go to the front fell as "martyrs."

The hawza has extensive endowments *(waqf,* pl. *auqâf),* and is therefore not financially dependent on the government. This independence is mentioned with pleasure, even toward the current political leadership in Tehran, to which the hawza does not have a tension-free relationship. After the death of Khomeinî, the administration was restructured. The hawza is presently run by a six-person "High Council" *(shûrâ-ye a'lâ).* Council members are elected by the teachers' general assembly and confirmed in office by the highest "source of imitation" *(marja' at-taqlîd)* and the leader of the revolution *(rahbar).* There are two commissions, responsible for curriculum and management, respectively.

Curriculum is divided into three levels. The lowest level is called the *muqaddamât* (Arabic for preparatory course). In addition to an introduction to Islamic law, Arabic is taught, which is the scholarly language of Islam and thus indispensable for the studies. A major portion of the traditional literature was written in Arabic and the Shi'i ulamâ throughout the world communicate through Arabic. This first level is completed by attaining a diploma after approximately four years (there are no strictly regimented academic years).

The second level is called *sat-h* (higher level) and includes study of the principles of Islamic jurisprudence and philosophy. After approximately five years, students graduate from this level with a "license" *(lisans)*.

Not until the third or "ending" *(khârij)* level are students trained to be qualified mujtahids. Students at this level wear a caftan and turban and work as a type of teaching assistant. This last segment of the course of study has neither a fixed length nor does it end with an examination. It is the task of the master teacher to closely observe students and declare when each of them is ready, awarding the "authorization" *(ijâza)* to perform the tasks of a mujtahid. Today there are approximately 300 mujtahids in Qom.[14] Teaching at the hawza has been greatly modernized over the last few years. English has long since become a standard language. In addition to traditional Islamic philosophy, knowledge of Western philosophers has recently been added to the curriculum. Kant and Hegel are currently very popular among the students.

Within the class of mujtahids, a kind of hierarchy has developed in recent years that is expressed through a standardized form of address. The first honorary title a mujtahid can attain is "authority of Islam and the Muslims" *(hujjat al-islâm wal-muslimîn);* President Rafsanjânî, for example, has this title. The next level is "sign of God" *(âyatu'llâh).* The highest title is "greatest sign of God" *(âyatu'llâh al-uzmâ);* this title is reserved for the very few grand âyatollâhs generally recognized as "sources of imitation" *(marja' at-taqlîd).* This honorary title is acquired in a rather informal manner: Mujtahids—if possessing the appropriate personal authority—are granted it by their own following. Either the form of address sticks or it is abandoned. No formal procedure of promotion has developed as yet in this rather new hierarchy.

14. Shi'i Revolutionary Ideology

Shi'ism is not revolutionary per se. For centuries it cultivated the ideal of suffering and endurance. The Shi'i prototype was that of the quietly enduring martyr *(shahîd)* and not the insurgent revolutionary. Attaining legitimate power through the successor of the Prophet according to the will of God remained the declared goal of Shi'ism, but this was reserved for the Hidden Imam. Until his return as the messianic Mahdî, believers had only to wait, pray, and hope. Traditional Shi'ism is apolitical and holding power has always raised suspicions. We have seen the reservations of the Shi'i ulamâ in serving even Shi'i potentates.

Revolutionary events in Iran have distorted outsiders' ability to see Shi'ism as quietistic. The leading ulamâ of the nineteenth and twentieth centuries, the great marja' at-taqlîd, have been almost exclusively nonpolitical to the present day: Shîrâzî (died 1895), Hâ'erî, the reformer of the school of Qom (died 1937), Borujerdî (died 1962), the book collector Mar'ashî (died 1991), Iraqi Grand Âyatollâh Khû'î (died 1992), or Grand Âyatollâh Golpâyegânî (1899-1993), who lived in seclusion in Qom until his death. They only occasionally intervened in current events, if the interests of the clergy or its paying following were directly affected, such as in the conflict over the tobacco concession or the land reform act of the last shah, which also affected a number of religious endowments.[15] The revolutionary Khomeinî was a "newcomer" among the grand âyatollâhs and his political agenda and activism raised suspicions among many of his conservative colleagues. He sought a role traditionally detested by members of the Shi'i clergy.

The conversion of Shi'i tradition into a revolutionary ideology is thus a very modern phenomenon and it demanded considerable modifications of the religious tradition. Such a transformation was essentially the work of westernized intellectuals and laypeople rather than religious figures. First and foremost in this effort were the Tehran teacher, ethnologist, and writer Jalâl Âl-e Ahmad (1923-1969) and his student, religious scholar and sociologist Alî Sharî'atî (1933-1977). Both were profoundly influenced by foreign, colonial rule and they experienced the Iranian people as exploited victims.

In a secret agreement in 1907, Russia and Great Britain divided up Iranian territory into spheres of interest. In the north, the Soviet Union later came into the colonial inheritance of Tsarist Russia, and after World War II the United States replaced Great Britain as the colonial power in the Gulf region. A CIA-backed coup d'état in 1953 brought an end to the national Iranian regime of Prime Minister Mosaddeq, who had nationalized the oil industry. Shah Mohammad Rezâ Pahlevî, who was reinstalled on the throne, maintained close ties to the United States. Resistance to these foreign influences is the true source of revolutionary Shi'ism, or the Shi'i revolution. It was the recent colonial past of the country that sowed the seeds of the intensely anti-Western attitudes of the Islamic revolution of 1979. These attitudes cannot be explained on the basis of traditional Islam in general nor Shi'i tradition in particular.

Âl-e Ahmad, former theology student *(talaba)* and—for a time—communist, developed into an ardent nationalist and xenophobe under the influence of Stalinist politics. He declared blind imitation of the West to be the reason why Iranians dissociated themselves from their own traditional values, cutting off the "roots," through which the lifeblood flowed into their culture. The title of his most well-known book made *gharb-zadagî*—a difficult word to translate—popular in Iran. In English it has been translated as "westoxication," "Euromania," "a plague from the West," and even "occidentosis": a terrible, fatal illness that has befallen the Iranian people.[16] Khomeinî later admitted that he read the book, published in 1962, with admiration. As a left-wing intellectual, Âl-e Ahmad could never totally overcome his skepticism of religion; nevertheless, he enthusiastically turned to his own religious tradition, which he saw as the only effective cure for the insidious plague. He felt religion was the only area not yet infected by the Western plague. Since a large majority of the Iranian people held fast to their religious traditions, he instinctually sensed a revolutionary potential in this area that could far surpass the potential among students and intellectuals influenced by Marxist ideology or the relatively small number of workers in the oilfields.

The impact of Âl-e Ahmad's books on an entire generation of Iranians, including theology students and the clergy, can hardly be overestimated. (The section that Roy Mottahedeh dedicated to Âl-e Ahmad in his book, *The Mantle of the Prophet,* offers an outstanding introduction into Âl-e Ahmad's ideas; a better illustration of the intellectual and spiritual atmosphere in Iran on the eve of the revolution could hardly be offered an outsider.)[17]

After Âl-e Ahmad's death in 1969, his ideas were taken up and developed further by Alî Sharî'atî in the 1970s. Like his predecessor, Sharî'atî was also the son of a preacher and raised in a strict, religious family at the shrine of Mashhad. But Sharî'atî studied religion and sociology in Paris (1960-65) and received a doctorate in Iranian philology from the Sorbonne.[18] He was influenced by Karl Marx and Max Weber, Jean Paul Sartre, Herbert Marcuse, and Frantz Fanon, the prophet of *négritude,* who was very popular at that time. Sharî'atî translated Fanon's book *The Damned of the Earth* into Persian. He developed his own ideology, which forced Western ideas and Iranian Shi'i tradition into a peculiar synthesis.[19] After returning to Iran, he was a teacher in an eastern Iranian village and then became an assistant professor at the University of Mashhad. Sharî'atî was dismissed for ideological reasons and went to Tehran, where he gave lectures at the "Husayniyya of Right Guidance *(Hoseyniyya-ye Ershâd)* from 1969 to 1973, a private religious academy that the shah closed down in 1973. After arrest, torture, and being placed under house arrest, Sharî'atî was able finally to leave Iran in 1977, but he died the same year in London.

Sharî'atî's form of Shi'ism is very unorthodox from the perspective of traditional mullahs.[20] He essentially developed a modern revolutionary ideology wrapped in traditional Shi'i images and symbols that he redefined and reassessed entirely. Shi'ism is defined as the struggle for justice against foreign rule, tyranny, feudalism, and exploitation. As soon as Shi'ism allies itself with ruling secular powers, it betrays its divine mission. For Sharî'atî, this fall from grace was manifested by the establishment of the Safavid monarchy in 1501. The greatest merit of Shi'ism up till then was their opposition to all dynasties that had established tyrannical regimes in the name of Islam. "Like a revolutionary party, Shi'ism had a well-organized, informed, deep and well-defined ideology, with clear-cut and definite slogans and a disciplined and well-groomed organization. It led the deprived and oppressed masses in their movements for freedom and for the seeking of justice."[21] Shi'ism in pre-Safavid times appeared "as the fountainhead of rebellion and the struggle of the downtrodden and oppressed masses, especially among the rural people." Sharî'atî celebrated as the first and last real Shi'i power the local Shi'i Sarbedârân dynasty of Sabzevâr (in northeastern Iran), which rebelled against the Mongol rule in the fourteenth century. "[F]or the first time, a revolutionary movement based on Alavite Shi'ism, against foreign domination, internal deceit, the power of the feudal lords and large capitalists, arises in arms for the salvation of the enslaved nation and the deprived masses, led by peasants seven hundred years ago, under the banner of justice and the culture of martyrdom." But a "century later came the Safavids and Shi'ism departed from the great mosque of the masses to become a next door neighbor to the Palace of 'Ali Qapu [and] the Royal Mosque [in Isfahân]. Red Shi'ism changes to Black Shi'ism. The religion of Martyrdom changes to the religion of Mourning."[22]

"Red Shi'ism" is "'Alawî," that is, the Shi'ism of the first imam, Alî; it is original, pure, true, unfalsified Shi'ism, Shi'ism of a revolutionary act and struggle against tyranny and exploitation. "Black Shi'ism" is "Safavid"; it accommodated itself among the powerful, the exploiters, the oppressors. It betrayed its revolutionary mission by replacing struggle and martyrdom with passive mourning at the Âshûrâ processions and weeping at the graves of the imams. Sharî'atî despised both the traditional Muharram rituals, with their self-flagellation and ta'ziyeh performances, and the juridical casuistry of the mullahs. He dreamed of an "Islam without clerics" *(islâm menhâ-ye âkhûnd).*[23] The mullahs and âyatollâhs, with their medieval volumes, their legal books, their commentaries and super commentaries, seemed to Sharî'atî to be an obstacle to knowledge, progress, and the revolutionary act. Earlier, his mentor Âl-e Ahmad had harshly criticized the mullahs in a similar fashion: "The religious establishment, with all its institutions and customs, leans on superstitions as much as it can. It seeks refuge in times long past and outdated ceremonies and is satisfied to be the gatekeeper at the graveyard."[24] This was an angry slur on traditional piety and the worshipping of the shrines of the imams.

A slogan that could often be read on banners in protest marches during the revolution came from Sharî'atî's work, *Martyrdom (Shahâdat):* "Karbalâ is everywhere; every month is Muharram; every day is Âshûrâ."[25] This revolutionary slogan contradicts all conventional interpretations. For traditional Shi'ites, Âshûrâ is precisely *not* every day, but only the 10th of Muharram. On the eleventh, traditional Shi'ites lie in bed with a bandaged head and on the twelfth, they are back at the bazaar selling onions. The ritualized self-sacrifice performed on Âshûrâ, described above (see p. 20) as the decisive step in the development of Shi'ism, is thus undone by Sharî'atî. Self-sacrifice is de-ritualized. Ritualized, substitute action—performed once a year with minimal bloodshed—is no longer sufficient. Every day is Âshûrâ and Karbalâ is everywhere. Martyrdom, sacrificial death, is demanded in service of the revolution (and later in service of the war against the Iraqi aggressors). Real death is permitted.

In addition to the de-ritualization of self-sacrifice, Sharî'atî also eliminated the eschatological expectation of the Mahdî. While the imams were present, God had given humanity a leader; since the disappearance of the twelfth imam, according to Sharî'atî, humanity as a whole has been commanded by God to act as a representative of the Hidden Imam and work to set up a just realm—not on some day in the future, but here and now. "Choose the vice-regency of the Imam to have a responsible leader," Sharî'atî appealed to his readers.[26] This negates the privileged role of the clergy, the qualified mujtahids. Sharî'atî felt that the masses themselves should establish the realm of the Mahdî. Religious endowments *(waqf,* plural *auqâf)* should be used "for the socio-political struggle, educational foundations and teaching." The religious authority of the "sources of imitation" *"(marja'iyye)"* should serve the "centralization of the [revolutionary] movement"; in the future, traditional "imitation" *(taqlîd)* should serve the revolutionary discipline. The old Shi'i practice of dissimulation *(taqiyya),* the denial of Shi'i beliefs in times of persecution, was reinterpreted into a conspiratorial activity of revolutionary cadres.

Like all twentieth-century Islamic ideologues, Sharî'atî also had an image of Islam that was ahistoric and utopian. Fourteen centuries of Islamic history were dismissed as an error. The image of a golden age, the era of the Prophet, of Fâtima, Alî, and the imams, was set against the path of history. "Shi'ites do not accept the path chosen by history," he says explicitly, and ". . . the present Islam [1972] is a criminal Islam in the dress of 'tradition' and. . . the real Islam is the hidden Islam, hidden in the red cloak of martyrdom."[27]

The de-ritualization of the Âshûrâ customs and the elimination of the eschatological expectation of the Mahdî are two major steps in transforming the traditional Shi'i religion into a revolutionary ideology. Âl-e Ahmad and Sharî'atî are the founding fathers of this ideology. Later, during Khomeinî's rule, some of their ideas were realized, even if the Âyatollâh harshly criticized the attacks of both authors against traditional clergy. The revolution took a different course than Âl-e Ahmad, Sharî'atî, and many of their supporters had imagined. Above all, they underestimated the power of the clergy, and developments thus quickly went beyond their expectations. Sharî'atî's ideas continue to survive in the underground movement of the left-wing, anti-clerical "jihâd fighters of the people" *(mujâhidîn-e khalq).*

15. Khomeinî and the "Government of the Expert"

Revolutions do not have religious causes; they develop out of economic, social, and political crises. In order to analyze them, it is necessary to use the methodological tools of sociologists, political scientists, and—as the events gradually move into the past—historians. This is just as true of the Iranian revolution as it is of all other revolutions in the last two hundred years. The fact that the Iranian revolution legitimized itself with a religious ideology surprised many Western observers simply because they were unfamiliar with it. This led them to come to the widespread, yet false conclusion that an attempt was being made to return to the Middle Ages.

Since this book is about the religion of the Shi'ites and not a socio-economic or historical analysis of the Islamic revolution in Iran, I shall merely mention some of the countless sources dealing specifically with this subject.[28] The political revolution also served to revolutionize Shi'ism itself and led to many essential changes, though it remains to be seen if they will be long-lived.

The most important innovation is the principle of "government of the expert" (Arabic: *wilâyat al-faqîh;* Persian: *velâyat-e faqîh),* developed theoretically by Khomeinî and then implemented in revolutionary practice. It has become the fundamental principle of the Islamic Republic of Iran and is laid down in the country's first constitution.

Rûhollâh Mûsavî Khomeinî was born in 1902 in Khomeyn (120 km southwest of Qom). He was a descendent of the seventh imam, Mûsâ al-Kâzim, which is why his true family name is *Mûsavî.* In 1918 he became a student of Âyatollâh Hâ'erî (see above, p. 129) in nearby Arâk and went with him to Qom in 1922, where he became a mujtahid in the 1930s and a teacher at the Feyziyya. Khomeinî's first book was written in 1943, when a number of Tehran bâzârîs pressured him to respond to attacks by anti-clerical secularists. The book was called "Revelation of the Secrets" *(Kashf al-asrâr);* it presented religion as the only guarantor of the country's independence and the ulamâ as a bastion against the shah's sell-out of Iranian interests to foreign powers. In it, Khomeinî harshly criticized Rezâ Shâh, who had be deposed two years earlier, yet he hoped to have a positive influence on Rezâ Shâh's young son and successor. Here, his attack on the monarchy was by no means as severe as it later became. In fact, he represented the traditional Shi'i standpoint in the question of participation of the mullahs in secular rule, which he thus saw as usurped. As long as serving the usurpers was in the interests of the Muslims, it was even seen as recommendable. Most importantly, the ulamâ was to support the rulers in defending the country against foreign influence and attacks.

The book dealt mainly with the role of the ulamâ or Islamic legal experts (fuqahâ, sing. faqîh) in a state. Since they alone know the revealed, legal order, or sharî'a, only they are in a position to decide what government actions are legal. "If we say that government and administration are the responsibilitiy of the [Islamic legal] experts, then we do not mean an expert (faqîh) must serve as shah, minister, general, or garbage collector. Much more we are saying . . . that a council (majlis) can be convened, made up of religious mujtahids who know the laws of God, are just and altruistic, have no other ambitions than to serve the good of the people and carry out divine law, and who could elect someone as a just ruler (sultân). . . . If there were an advisory council made up of or supervised by religious experts, what in the world would be wrong with that?"[29]

With this statement, Khomeinî was following the tradition of Article 2 of the amendment to the Iranian constitution of 1907 (see above, p. 126). It provided for a body of Islamic legal experts to monitor the legislation of the parliament. This did not yet call for a direct takeover of power by the mullahs; they were merely called upon to control the monarch and his officials. In carrying out this task, the mullahs function as a collective; the constitution does not provide for a specially qualified and empowered "leader."[30]

Khomeinî's position quickly radicalized in reaction to the politics of Shah Mohammad Rezâ Pahlavî. He became a relentless opponent of the monarch and the monarchy. His resistance was sparked primarily by the reforms the shah referred to as the "white revolution," which he wanted to have confirmed by referendum in 1963. The most important point in this reform program was the land reform act. Anyone whose interests were restricted by this law—including many members of the clergy and their following[31]—saw Khomeinî as their unrelenting spokesman and leader. The repressiveness of the shah's regime drove students in Qom to the streets: on Âshûrâ 1963 (June 5), riots started that were then brutally suppressed. In October of the following year, Khomeinî made an open stand against the shah's plans to give diplomatic status to the numerous U.S. military advisors he had brought into the country. Khomeinî accurately compared such an act to the "capitulations," the special rights that the Qajar shahs had granted foreign colonial powers. The real motivation behind "Khomeinî the revolutionary'"s actions were his anti-colonial attitudes, which were already noticeable in his first book. These attitudes then took on clear form. The secret of his success was that his opinions were shared by many, predominantly younger, intellectuals who were impressed by his uncompromising behavior.

Khomeinî had dared to openly call the shah the "Yazîd of our time"—an insinuation that was understandable and obvious to all Shi'ites. Caliph Yazîd was the ruler responsible for the massacre at Karbalâ. Khomeinî was arrested and deported to Turkey. In October 1965, however, he had already settled at the shrine of an-Najaf in Iraq, where he once again gathered a circle of students and gave sermons to Iranian pilgrims. Audio cassettes with recordings of his speeches were very popular.

In an-Najaf, Khomeinî wrote his second major polemic, *The Islamic Government* (Arabic: *al-Hukûma al-islâmiyya;* Persian: *Hokûmat-e eslâmî),* which developed out of a lecture he had held in January and February 1970 for his scholastic circle.[32] Excluding the numerous Quran verses and citations from sayings of the Prophet and the imams, this treatise is basically an anti-colonialist appeal:

"That is our situation then—created for us by the foreigners through their propaganda and their agents. They have removed from operation all the judicial processes and political laws of Islam and replaced them with European importations, thus diminishing the scope of Islam and ousting it from Islamic society. For the sake of exploitation they have installed their agents in power.

"So far, we have sketched the subversive and corrupting plan of imperialism. We must now take into consideration as well certain internal factors, notably the dazzling effect that the material progress of the imperialist countries has had on some members of our society.

". . . . The imperialists have propagated among us the view that Islam does not have a specific form of government or governmental institutions. They say further that even if Islam does have certain laws, it has no method for enforcing them, so that its function is purely legislative. This kind of propaganda forms part of the overall plan of the imperialists to prevent the Muslims from becoming involved in political activity and establishing an Islamic government.

". . . . The imperialists began laying their plans three or four centuries ago; they started out with nothing, but see where they are now! We too will begin with nothing, and we will pay no attention to the uproar created by a few 'xenomaniacs' (gharbzadaha) and devoted servants of imperialism.

"Present Islam to the people in its true form, so that our youth do not picture the akhunds as sitting in some corner in Najaf or Qum, studying the questions of menstruation and parturition instead of concerning themselves with politics, and draw the conclusion that religion must be separate from politics. This slogan of the separation of religion and politics and the demand that Islamic scholars not intervene in social and political affairs have been formulated and propagated by the imperialists; it is only the irreligious who repeat them. Were religion and politics separate in the time of the Prophet (peace and blessings be upon him)? Did there exist, on one side, a group of clerics, and opposite it, a group of politicians and leaders? Were religion and politics separate in the time of the caliphs—even if they were not legitimate—or in the time of the Commander of the Faithful (upon whom be peace)? Did two separate authorities exist? These slogans and claims have been advanced by the imperialists and their political agents in order to prevent religion from ordering the affairs of this world and shaping Muslim society, and at the same time to create a rift between the scholars of Islam, on the one hand, and the masses and those struggling for freedom and independence, on the other. They have thus been able to gain dominance over our people and plunder our resources, for such has always been their ultimate goal.

"If we Muslims do nothing but engage in the canonical prayer, petition God, and invoke His name, the imperialists and the oppressive governments allied with them will leave us alone. If we were to say, 'Let us concentrate on calling the *azan* and saying our prayers. Let them come rob us of everything we own—God will take care of them! There is no power or recourse except in Him, and God willing, we will be rewarded in the hereafter!'—if this were our logic, they would not disturb us.

"Once, during the occupation of Iraq, a certain British officer asked: 'Is the *azan* I hear being called now from the minaret harmful to British policy?' When he was told that it was harmless, he said: 'Then let him call for prayer as much as he wants!"[33]

Khomeinî's anti-colonialist tirade—like that of most members of the clergy in his generation—is primarily anti-British. It was influenced by the experience of British politics in Iran and Iraq prior to World War II, but after the war the target was smoothly transferred to the United States, which now appeared at the Gulf as the guardian of Western interests. The entire treatise shows that Khomeinî wanted to do away with quietistic Shi'ism that was oriented toward the Judgment Day and the hereafter. Waiting meekly for the return of the Hidden Imam was to be replaced by the revolutionary act.

The monarchy was declared anti-Islamic and even blasphemous. This did not apply only to the Pahlavî regime, but to monarchy per se: "Islam proclaims monarchy and hereditary succession wrong and invalid. When Islam first appeared in Iran, the Byzantine Empire, Egypt, and the Yemen, the entire institution of monarchy was abolished. In the blessed letters that the Most Noble Messenger (peace and blessings be upon him) wrote to the Byzantine Emperor Heraclius and the Shahanshah of Iran, he called upon them to abandon the monarchical and imperial form of government, to cease compelling the servants of God to worship them with absolute obedience. . . ."[34] The struggle of al-Husayn at Karbalâ is interpreted in the same way as a struggle against the non-Islamic principle of monarchy. The imam could have paid homage to the Umayyad caliph, thereby acknowledging the ruling dynasty, but he did not compromise himself to the monarch and preferred to sacrifice himself in the battle—as a model for future generations.

The imams were also fighters; they wore chain mail and helmets and carried a sword (even if like the fifth imam they did not always have the opportunity to prove their will to go to battle). But what happened during the occultation (ghayba) of the imam? "In order to clarify the matter further, let us pose the following questions: From the time of the Lesser Occultation down to the present (a period of more than twelve centuries that may continue for hundreds of millenia if it is not appropriate for the Occulted Imam to manifest himself), is it proper that the laws of Islam be cast aside and remain unexecuted, so that everyone acts as he pleases and anarchy prevails?"[35]

The kingdom of justice of the imam must be represented and anticipated by the "government of the expert" (Arabic: wilâyat al-faqîh, Persian: velâyat-e faqîh), i.e., government of a qualified scholar who knows the divine revelation and God's will. It does not matter whether Khomeinî used the singular faqîh as a collective noun or in reference to a particular person—such as himself. At any rate, the latter was the de facto result after the revolution. Up to that time, the scholars *(al-ulamâ)* or experts *(al-fuqahâ,* singular: *al-faqîh)*—the two terms are synonymous —had control over government measures at most. They wanted to keep an eye on the secular arm. But the term *wilâya* means "exercise of rule"; the principle newly formulated by Khomeinî referred to the direct rule by the clergy in the absence of another Islamic government:

"Now that this much has been demonstrated, it is necessary that the *fuqaha* proceed, collectively or individually, to establish a government in order to implement the laws of Islam and protect its territory. If this task falls within the capabilities of a single person, he has personally incumbent upon him the duty to fulfill it; otherwise, it is a duty that devolves upon the *fuqaha* as a whole. Even if it is impossible to fulfill the task, the authority vested in the *fuqaha* is not voided, because it has been vested in them by God. If they can, they must collect taxes, such as *zakât, khums,* and *kharaj,* spend them for the welfare of the Muslims, and also enact the penalties of the law [as stated in the Quran]."[36]

Khomeinî was not interested in preserving the centuries-old, traditional system of Shi'ism. On the contrary, he wanted to replace it with something totally new. The passage about the use of the *khums* (see above, p. 91-94) clearly shows this. The legally permitted income may not—as was previously the case—be used to support the descendents of the Prophet *(sayyids),* but must serve the general good:

". . . . If an Islamic government is achieved, it will have to be administered on the basis of the taxes that Islam has established—*khums, zakât* (this, of course, would not represent an appreciable sum), *jizya,* and *kharaj.*

"How could the *sayyids* ever need so vast a budget? The *khums* of the bazaar of Baghdad would be enough for the needs of the *sayyids* and the upkeep of the religious teaching institution, as well as all the poor people of the Islamic world, quite apart from the *khums* of the bazaars of Tehran, Istanbul, Cairo, and other cities. The provision of such a huge budget must obvi-

ously be for the purpose of forming a government and administering the Islamic lands. It was established with the aim of pro-
viding for the needs of the people, for public services relating to
health, education, defense, and economic development. . . .

"Now, should we cast this huge treasury into the ocean, or
bury it until the Imam returns, or just spend it on fifty *sayyids*
a day until they have all eaten their fill? Let us suppose we give
all this money to 500,000 *sayyids;* they would not know what to
do with it. We all know that the *sayyids* and the poor have a
claim on the public treasury [according to Quran 8.41] only to
the extent required for subsistence."[37]

It is the "masters' share" *(sahm-e sâdât)* that is being ques-
tioned here, that is, the half of the *khums* that according to Shi'i
law is supposed to benefit not the imam, but the members of the
large, extended family of the Prophet (see above, p. 92). Their
claims are set against the general welfare of the Muslims. Such
ideas break down the foundation for the traditional interest in
caring for the sayyids, as expressed by major segments of the
religious establishment. Khomeinî thus revolutionized not only
the Iranian state, but traditional Shi'ism as well.

16. The Leader of the Revolution

The figure of a charismatic, quasi infallible leader fits in with
the image of revolution in the twentieth century—from Lenin to
the *Great Helmsman* Mao to the *Máximo Líder* Fidel Castro.
The outstanding position of the Âyatollâh Khomeinî had less to
do with the religious tradition of the Shi'ites as with his role as
revolutionary. However, he benefitted from the trend that had
started last century toward the formation of a hierarchy of Shi'i
clergy. The intermittent but widespread acknowledgement of
one individual Grand Âyatollâh as the "source of imitation"
(marja' at-taqlîd) could now be institutionalized in the service of
the revolution. The ways in which this was done are just as

innovational as the absolute authority that the leader of the revolution claimed for himself.

Khomeinî's prestige as a relentless opponent of the shah received widespread acceptance from a broad opposition including left-wing, bourgeois liberals and religious laypeople, and a variety of moderate and radical clerical groups. The revolution began when liberal politician Shâhpûr Bakhtiyâr, a member of the *National Front* founded by Mosaddeq, demanded in 1977 that the Iranian constitution of 1906-07 be reestablished. In Qom and elsewhere, theology students took to the streets. When the military shot into a mass demonstration on September 8, 1978 and hundreds died, the violent riots could no longer be restrained.

Âyatollâh Khomeinî followed and tried to control the events from his exile in an-Najaf. A month later he was banished from Iraq at the instigation of the shah and settled in Neauphle-le-Château in France (30 km west of Paris), where he publicly demanded the elimination of the monarchy and the establishment of an Islamic republic based on the principle of the "government of the expert." A mass demonstration following the Âshûrâ processions on December 12, 1978 took up this cause. On January 16, 1979 the shah left the country after declaring the leader of the secular bourgeois opposition, Bakhtiyâr, head of the government. But the revolution soon went far beyond this. Khomeinî landed in Tehran on February 1st. Engineer Mahdî Bâzargân, a strict, religious layperson, formed a provisional revolutionary government; Bakhtiyâr gave up the struggle and left the country. Only a month after his arrival, Khomeinî settled in Qom.

In the constitution of the Islamic Republic that was approved by referendum on December 2-3, 1979, sovereignty was granted not to the people but to God (Article 56); the Hidden Imam was declared the only legitimate representative of God on earth. "During the occultation of the Hidden Imam—may God speed his return!—the authority of government *(vilâyat-e amr)* and leadership of the community *(imâmat-e ummat)* shall lie with the just, pious, contemporary, and bold experts authorized for leadership and guidance *(faqîh)*, whom a majority of the population has called to leadership *(rahbarî)* and confirmed (Article 5). Article 107 mentions "the Grand Âyatollâh Khomeinî" by name as the current leader *(rahbar)*. "Should no Islamic legal scholar achieve a majority, a leadership council *(shûrâ-ye rahbarî)* of Islamic legal scholars who satisfy the above prerequisites shall assume leadership in accordance with Article 107" (Article 5).

In addition to the leader or leadership council, a supervisory council *(shûrâ-ye negahbân)* of six religious, legal scholars and six secular jurists has the task of monitoring all laws passed by the parliament *(majles)* to assure that they comply with the revealed, divine order (Article 4); this is a revised version of Article 2 of the constitutional amendment of 1907.

The official religion of the Islamic Republic of Iran is Islam of the Twelver Shi'i *(ja'faritic)* faith; the four Sunni "schools" are unconditionally recognized (Article 12); "Iranian citizens of the Zoroastrian, Jewish, and Christian faiths are recognized as official religious minorities" (Article 13); these are the traditional "charges" *(dhimmîs)* of classical Islamic law and they enjoy full protection of the Sharî'a. Shaykhî, Bâbî, and Bahâ'î, religious communities that evolved out of Shi'ism, are not mentioned; their members are considered apostates and are thus victims of persecution.

It is not possible to describe the course of the revolution in detail here. In any case, Khomeinî and his closest supporters succeeded in eliminating the other wings of the broadly based opposition one by one. The first prime minister, Bâzargân, and the first president, Banî Sadr—both laypeople from the religious camp—were deprived of their powers and overthrown. The war against Iraq (1981-88) strengthened Khomeinî's position.

There is no model in traditional Shi'ism for the office of political leader *(rahbar)*. It is a revolutionary innovation. The referendum on the constitution—which is also new—served to confirm what was a kind of plebiscitary *de facto* imamate for Khomeinî. Article 5 expressly refers to the "imamate of the umma," which the leader assumes on behalf of the Hidden Imam. Even if he never actually referred to himself as an imam, Khomeinî nevertheless played the role of an imam number 11b. His supporters raised the status of his directives—through which he influenced political events in a more informal manner—to that of quasi infallibility. Although his directives were labelled expert opinions *(fatwâ)*, they were actually something qualitatively new and different. A traditional *fatwâ* is nothing more than the private opinion of a legal expert who can very well be contradicted by another expert. No believer of the faith is obliged to follow a specific *fatwâ*. Directives by the "leader," however, do not have the same unbinding character. They are authoritative and demand absolute obedience.

This also applies to the *fatwâ* of February 14, 1989 against author Salman Rushdie. It called not only for Rushdie, as author of *The Satanic Verses,* to be killed, but his publishers too. My intention is not to speculate about specific reasons that existed at the time, such as the need to find a new "Great Satan," after the July 1988 cease-fire with Iraq, which Khomeinî disapproved of. Muslim theologues and jurists debate the question of "apostasy" *(ridda* or *irtidâd)* with respect to Rushdie (the Sunni authorities at Azhar University in Cairo and the international Organization of Islamic Conference criticized Khomeinî's conduct) at a merely superficial level. Irrespective of the claim of the leader of the Iranian revolution to be able to make such a binding judgment in the name of the entire Islamic world, the Rushdie case is not an example of classical apostasy. It could easily be dismissed by a traditional Shi'i mujtahid since Rushdie was raised as a Sunni. According to Shi'i doctrine, only Shi'ites can be regarded as true believers, whereas those who never had true faith cannot break it; they will not be able to avoid God's judgment anyway.

The real point here, however, is that in the eyes of his adversaries, Rushdie never converted from Islam to Christianity or any other religion; rather, he converted to the "West," which is his true crime. Those who wish to see him die view him as the incarnation of that which writer Âl-e Ahmad characterized in 1962 as "occidentosis" *(gharb-zadagî)*, that deadly disease of alienation, and they are terrified of being infected. To them, Rushdie is not a Muslim who became a Christian; he is a Muslim who became British. He lives there, writes English, and earns British pounds sterling while playing a frivolous game with the sacred traditions of Islam. He is the Muslim who collaborates with the colonialists. His "treason" is primarily political and not religious. The Indian Muslims in England who denounced Rushdie to Khomeinî, in particular, will never tire of characterizing him as a hired agent of the "West." The author was thus stylized into a symbol of the anti-colonial struggle and made into a scapegoat for much frustration and hatred. He became an incarnation of evil per se. A book published in Iran even shows him as having the grotesque face and horns of a devil. An extensive propaganda campaign was responsible for spreading this demonic image of Rushdie. Although it no longer has much to do either with the author or his works, such an image is hard to shake. It is difficult to imagine that an Iranian government following the heritage of Khomeinî would want to or would be in a position to compromise the deceased âyatollâh in this central aspect of revolutionary doctrine, least of all in response to pressure from a Western government. That would be admitting capitulation to the very "West" against whom the revolution was fought. The occupation of the U.S. embassy in November 1979 and the judgment against Salman Rushdie were both intentional violations of Western norms—as imposed by the West—committed with the intention of terminating them. And this is indeed how both were received in the West.

Khomeinî's revolutionary supporters stressed his quasi infallibility even more definitively after his death on June 3, 1989. His successor, Khâmene'î, renewed the judgment and in June 1990, Husayn Mûsaviyyân, responsible for Europe and America in the Iranian foreign ministry, declared that "neither I nor any other Iranian dignitary nor the state of Iran itself has the power to reverse this decision." The traditional principle of "the deceased have no authority" *(lâ qawla li 'l-mayyit)* is thus no longer in force. The absolute authority of the leader of the revolution has retained its validity even after his death.

Khomeinî's virtually imam-like position is manifested especially in his mausoleum south of Tehran. Its gold-bronze metal dome and steel minarets are an obvious replica of the shrine of al-Husayn in Karbalâ, though in larger proportions. Rituals common at the graves of the imams are performed at the grave of the *rahbar* as well. Reference has already been made to the Iranian prisoners of war who, upon their release from Iraq, bewailed their shame for not having died in service to the deceased âyatollâh. The iconography of revolutionary propaganda has clearly borrowed from traditional images of popular portrayals of the martyrdom at Karbalâ. In particular, the willingness to self-sacrifice and martyrdom, as has been preached for centuries, were instrumentalized for the revolution and the war against the Iraqi aggressors.

17. Illustrating Ijtihâd Using the Example of Birth Control

In theory, the position of the leader of the revolution is no different from that of a traditional mujtahid. He makes decisions on the basis of rational judgment *(ijtihâd)* to the best of his knowledge and belief.

This process can be demonstrated using the example of birth control. Iran and many other countries in the Islamic world have been confronted with serious problems stemming from rapid population growth. There were 22 million people in Iran in 1963; by 1979 the population had already grown to 34 million. The growth rate from 1980-1990 was 3.6%, which means that the annual population rise during this period was over a million. In 1990 Iran's population had already reached 57 million.

As in all Islamic countries, having a lot of children is traditionally regarded as a divine blessing. Reservations felt by most of the Shi'i ulamâ toward artificial means of birth control were shared by a majority of the population at large.

In 1979, the year of the revolution, demographic problems were already so pronounced that the first minister of health of the Islamic Republic of Iran raised the issue of permitting contraceptives to the *rahbar* Khomeinî. Khomeinî made a formal decision like that of a classical mujtahid. The result of his ijtihâd was publicized in the Iranian media and reprinted many times. At the same time, the press attempted to present the principle that led to Khomeinî's decision.

"Imam Khomeini in his verdict said: regarding religious legitimacy to use contraceptives, provided that from the health point of view, it should not be hazardous to women and application methods should be with the consent of husbands. Thus Iranian couples who wanted smaller families were free to do so.

"It should also be noted that throughout the Holy Qur'an, there is no stipulation whatsoever, prohibiting family planning and application of contraception. To the contrary, there are a number of verses, unrelated directly to family planning and revealed to Prophet Muhammad (peace be upon him) on other issues, which signify family planning.

"In this regard, Verse 233 from 'Baghareh' (the Cow) chapter of the holy Qur'an says: 'Mothers should breast feed their children two full years provided they want to complete the nursing. The family head must support women and clothe them properly, yet no person is charged with more than he can cope with. No mother should be made to suffer because of her child, nor any family head because of his child.'

"The strict observance of instructions in the above mentioned verse concerning breast feeding for two full years, is in itself a kind of contraception and will minimize the possibility of early pregnancy. Therefore, application of the aforesaid recommendations will lead to a decline in fertility and birth spacing.

"Some Islamic scholars have a more broader interpretation of the said Quranic verse. They believe that the stipulation 'No mother should be made to suffer because of her child, nor any family head because of his child' is yet another evidence that implies family planning.

"Based on the Baghareh chapter, some scholars also say that on the one hand the pregnancy of a woman is only permissible if first of all she is physically ready for pregnancy and second that the child should not deprive the mother of having a decent life. Furthermore, the father should have the sufficient means to support the child.

"So it can be said that Islam's support for more children is not everlasting, it may be subject to the mental, physical and economic conditions of parents.

"The application of various methods of contraception has been discussed by Muslim jurists, scientists and scholars who have generally concluded that methods not harmful to women is permissible."[38]

The birth rate in Iran today is only 3.2% and is going down. This example of a classical ijtihâd shows how flexible and adaptable Shi'i law is in principle. The first fatwâ of Khomeinî's successor Khâmene'î, for example, declared the transplantation of organs from persons who are brain-dead to be permissible. The method of ijtihâd need not serve to cement conservative or reactionary positions; it can also be used as an instrument of change. It depends on who uses this instrument and to what end.

18. The Successor to the Rahbar

Khomeinî's rule was absolute and unconditional. His word was law. President of the parliament Khâmane'î, who later became his successor, had reason to tell critics that "it is a misleading interpretation to say that the faqîh acts in his own interests and is a dictator. Someone who acts in the name of God is not a dictator."

Unlike other absolute rulers in similar positions, Âyatollâh Khomeinî took charge of designating his successor at a very early point in time. The 1979 referendum on the constitution served more to confirm Khomeinî in office than actually elect him. Articles 107 and 108 provided for an assembly of experts to choose a successor. A law was to determine the actual members of the assembly, which was made up of 61 (later 74) mujtahids, elected for eight years. In 1985 the assembly had already designated Âyatollâh Husayn Alî Montazerî, a former student of Khomeinî, to be the future rahbar. Since he evidently did not totally support Khomeinî's hard line, he was dropped in March 1989 and he stepped down. No new successor was designated, but Khomeinî initiated a commission only a month later, which was supposed to revise the constitution. The revised constitution did not go into force, however, until after Khomeinî's death (on June 3).

Essentially, the changes implemented by the new constitution dealt with the position of the president and the rahbar. The office of prime minister was eliminated. The president assumed leadership of the government, thereby taking on a clearly strengthened position of power. The modifications concerning the role of the leader of the revolution were more significant. Bâzargân, the first revolutionary head of the Iranian government, once characterized the "government of the expert" *(velây-at-e faqîh)* as a robe tailored to fit only Khomeinî. Khomeinî evidently saw things that way himself. In the year before his death, he tried to redefine the qualifications for the future rahbar. He himself had brought together political leadership with the religious authority of a "source of imitation" *(marja' at-taqlîd)*. This was reflected in the old constitution through the formulation: "[religious] authority and leadership" *(marja'iyyat va rahbarî)* (Article 105). It was problematic to make this combination, custom-made for Khomeinî, into a future prerequisite for the office of leader of the revolution. The authority of a marja' is usually attained at a very late age. Most marja's are over eighty or ninety years old. In addition, most of them were apolitical scholars. More than just a few were extremely reserved with respect to Khomeinî's revolutionary course, if not totally opposed to it. Khomeinî himself was thus in favor of separating religious authority *(marja'iyyat)* and revolutionary leadership *(rahbarî)* in the future. In a letter to the members of the commission to revise the constitution, he wrote: "From the very beginning, I believed and insisted that the *[marja'iyyat]* should not be a qualification for leadership . . . but [our] colleagues insisted . . . and I accepted it. I knew then [when the first constitution was being drafted—H.H.] that. . . it cannot be implemented. It is sufficient to have a just *mojtahed* [as a leader—H.H.], who is selected by the Assembly of Experts, . . . whose decrees then must be obeyed."[39]

Some members of the commission objected to Khomeinî's directive. They thought it questionable that religious authority would again fall to a number of marja's whose informal authority was based on spontaneous recognition by their following, thus making it extremely difficult to subject it to government influence and control. It was even a greater problem that any marja' could counter the rahbar's directives with a fatwâ, since the rahbar was only a simple mujtahid. This could easily make a marja' into a mouthpiece—or even a puppet—of oppositional groups. But Khomeinî was unwavering. The revised constitution provided that the rahbar did not necessarily have to have achieved the status of a marja'. The election of the leader by the Iranian people was also no longer mentioned in the new constitution.

The question of finding a successor became acute before the revision of the constitution was completed. Khomeinî died on June 3, 1989. On the next day, the assembly of experts already convened and elected—60 ayes and 14 nays—the former president of the parliament, Sayyid Alî Khâmene'î (born 1940) to be the provisional rahbar. He was then confirmed in office once the revised constitution went into effect. Khâmene'î was a muj-tahid, but he had the title of a *hujjat al-islâm* (see p. 131 above), i.e., he was not even an âyatollâh. In order to reinforce his authority, the speaker of the parliament, members of the assembly of experts, and Imâm Kâshânî, Friday preacher from Tehran, all declared it a religious obligation to obey the new rahbar unconditionally. On the same day that Khâmene'î was elected rahbar, the over-90-year-old Âyatollâh Arâkî was pro-claimed a new marja'. The political and religious authority that Khomeinî combined was thus divided between two people. In his first fatwâ, the new marja' declared that the imitation *(taqlîd)* of a deceased mujtahid was indeed permissible.[40] With that, the old principle, "the deceased have no authority" *(lâ qawla li 'l-mayyit),* was annulled as far as Khomeinî was con-cerned, and thus the authority of the leader of the revolution could be applied even after his death and played off against any possible ijtihâd of the opposition; this, too, was a revolutionary innovation.

These complex regulations were implemented hastily in the first few days after Khomeinî's death. They show how precari-ous the situation was during the transition from the former to the new leader. President Rafsanjânî and Rahbar Khâmene'î were nevertheless able to stabilize their power and, in coopera-tion, increase it.

The relationship between directives of the former and the present rahbar remains unclear: Can the new rahbar overturn decisions of the former? Khomeinî's closest supporters are try-ing as best they can to reinforce the authority of the deceased rahbar and prevent any deviation from his course. In the case of Rushdie, Khâmene'î had to confirm the fatwâ although he had spoken out for a conciliatory solution while Khomeinî was still alive. The political background to the case has been described above. In some other cases, fatwâs of the new rahbar clearly modified previous decisions, even if this was done very cautiously and regarding rather marginal issues. The political leadership has to pay attention to the opinions of the radical fol-

lowers of Khomeinî. Khomeinî's strict verdict against all forms
of music was largely annulled in May 1992 and the ban on production, use, and export of caviar was even expressly revoked.

The caviar fatwâ shows once again how ijtihâd functions.
Khomeinî declared not only caviar—an important Iranian
export article—and sturgeon, its "source," to be harâm (prohibited), but swordfish as well, a common food on the Gulf coast.
His justification was that both sturgeon and swordfish are "fish
without scales." Shi'ites have not been allowed to eat fish without scales since time immemorial, similar to the prohibition to
eating pork. Since both of these fishes have skin, Khomeinî for-
bid their being eaten, for purely religious reasons. The beluga
fishing fleets in the Caspian Sea were laid up and the caviar
factories closed. After Khomeinî's death, however, science made
considerable progress. The Iranian press immediately reported
that scientists from the National Fisheries Organization had
discovered "microscopic scales" on both sturgeon and swordfish.
This paved the way for a new fatwâ. Meanwhile, the official
"tourist guide for Iran" advertises "Fresh Iranian Caviar" with
a color photograph of an appetizing plate of caviar on the back
cover.

To some extent, Khâmene'î has been raised to the status of an
âyatollâh and marja' by virtue of his office. After the death of
the marja' Arâkî in December 1994, the attempt failed to have
Rahbar Khâmene'î honored as the highest religious authority
(marja' at-taqlîd) (see above, p. 122). Khâmene'î has since been
regarded as an undisputed âyatollâh, but the question of the
revolutionary leader's religious authority has by no means been
clarified once and for all; it will be posed anew when
Khâmene'î's successor takes office.

19. The Shi'ites as a Party in the Middle East Conflicts

A broad public sphere in the West did not concern itself with the Shi'ites until they started interfering in various conflicts in the Middle East. Hardly anyone took note of the Shi'ites prior to the Iranian revolution in 1979. This is partly because, outside Iran, the Shi'ites are usually a minority without any political significance. They did not even play an important role in national politics in Iraq, where the Shi'i population is larger than that of the Sunnis.

The fact that the Shi'ites belonged to the underprivileged in most countries has led directly to their being at the front line of power struggles in the Middle East for more than a decade. For them this is a struggle against underdevelopment, discrimination, and oppression; it is a battle for a place in the sun, a piece of the pie. The segmentary oriental society has had a centuries-old tradition of religiously defined groups speaking out in solidarity on certain issues; religious groups are also social ones. This is often not apparent to Western observers who, for example, misinterpreted the Lebanese civil war as simply a war between different religious groups. In reality, social groups were fighting for a redistribution of power in Lebanon, which was in the process of collapsing. Involved in the struggle were Christian Maronites, Sunni Muslims, Druzes, and—somewhat later—the Shi'ites in South Lebanon.

The segmentation of societies in the Middle East is not exclusively manifested in religiously defined groups. Ethnic, linguistic differentiation also plays an important and sometimes more significant role. The Kurds are Sunnis, as are their adversaries in Turkey and Iraq; but they speak a different language. The warring parties in the civil war in Afghanistan are basically ethnic groups, i.e., the Pashtuns, Turkish Uzbeks, Iranian Tajiks, and the Mongol (Shi'i) Hezâra. In Lebanon, on the other hand, there is no ethnic differentiation between the conflicting parties; they are all Arabs.

The ethnic and religious affiliations of a group sometimes coincide, e.g., Azeris are Turkish-speaking Shi'ites (or Shi'i Turks). This is not the rule, however. Like the Sunni population in central Iraq, the peasant population in southern Iraq is Arab, but it is Shi'i, like the Iranians, who speak a different language. Their political loyalties are predetermined on the basis of neither ethnic nor religious affiliation, nor are they immutable. When Iraq declared war on Iran in September 1980, some Western observers predicted that, on the basis of their religious faith, the Iraqi Shi'ites would flock to the Iran side. When this did not occur—even though among Iraqi soldiers, who had the greatest opportunity to defect, there was a large proportion of Shi'ites—it was explained by the "eternal hostilities" between Arabs and Persians. This second conclusion proved to be just as inaccurate as the first. After the Gulf War in 1991, the Shi'ites of southern Iraq revolted against the regime in Baghdad— Arabs versus Arabs—and looked to Iran for backing. The speculation that Iran planned to intervene militarily in southern Iraq also never came to be. Iran had good reasons—political, economic, and military—to avoid a second war with Iraq, although it triggered open disappointment from some Shi'i leaders.

In Azerbaijan as well, religious faith does not determine attitudes with respect to foreign policy. One must bear in mind that in the former Soviet republic of Azerbaijan, there were only 5 million Shi'i Âzerîs (in a total population of 7 million), but in the Iranian province directly to the south there were 12 million. These 17 million Âzerîs are Shi'ites, but they are also Turks. Their language is closely related to the Turkish spoken in Turkey. When the Soviet Union started to collapse, expectations were expressed that the Âzerî Shi'ites would seek close contact to Shi'i Iran. Rash commentators already imagined the border along the Aras River disappearing from the map. But a few posters with a portrait of Khomeinî do not make an Islamic revolution. Azerbaijan oriented itself more toward its neighbor Turkey, which brought with it a revival of Pan-Turkish fantasies. Nationalism also grew in Azerbaijan itself, even daring to bring forth dreams of a Greater Azerbaijan, including the northwestern province of Iran. It is obvious, however, that whoever is in power in Tehran would not tolerate a second, major Turkish state along Iran's northern border. Moreover, the Iranian province of Azerbaijan is one of the most highly industrialized regions of Iran, whereas the former Soviet republic is very poor. The Âzerî population in Tabrîz (Iran) does not necessarily want to be ruled by the Âzerîs of Baku (Azerbaijan). The most recent development in Azerbaijan politics, however—the wavering between Russia and the United States—goes to show that surprises must always be reckoned with in the region.

Religious affiliation thus does not always determine the political orientation of the Shi'ites. Iran comes to the aid of Shi'ites in neighboring countries in order to increase its influence and thus further its aim of assuming a leadership role in the Middle East—Iran's military aid of the militant Hizbollâh (Party of God) in Lebanon is the best example. Shi'ites have nothing against receiving support from their Big Brother in Iran as long as it is in their own interest. But Iran's financial and military means are not unlimited. In addition, Iran is itself a multiethnic state and the border areas are populated entirely by non-Iranians (Âzerîs in the north and Arabs in the southwest) and even non-Shi'ites (Kurds, Turkomans, Baluchis); politics aiming to destabilize the existing territorial states could thus backfire on the fragile Iran.

The subject here is more religion than politics, but it is very difficult in this case to separate the two. Most Shi'i political leaders are members of the clergy. In keeping with ancient Shi'i tradition, the highest Shi'i dignitary in Iraq, the highly esteemed Grand Âyatollâh Khû'î (died 1992), did not get involved in politics, which foiled Saddam Hussein's attempts to gain his favor. Other leading ulamâ, on the other hand, called upon the Shi'ites to resist the regime in political and armed struggle. Many were true to Shi'i tradition and became martyrs. Âyatollâh Sayyid Muhammad Bâqir as-Sadr was executed in

1980 along with his sister. At least twenty-two members of the al-Hakîm ulamâ family were executed or murdered. One of the survivors, Muhammad Bâqir al-Hakîm (born 1938), a son of Âyatollâh Muhsin al-Hakîm, who died in 1970 (see above, p. 121), went into exile in Tehran in 1980 with his brother. From there he led the protest of the Shi'ites of southern Iraq in early 1991. The rebellion was bloodily suppressed by Saddam Hussein. The holy cities of the Shi'ites—Karbalâ and an-Najaf—were drawn into the struggles and the shrines desecrated.

Sayyid Mûsâ as-Sadr, an Iranian cleric of Arab-Lebanese descent, was born in 1928 as the son of a mujtahid in Qom. Starting in 1951, he assumed the spiritual leadership of the Shi'ites in southern Lebanon and led the Shi'ites to a position of power in the country. He founded *Amal* (hope), the political, military organization of the Shi'ites, and disappeared without a trace in 1978 when his flight to Italy had a stopover in Tripoli, in Libya.

The other Lebanese Shi'i organization, the militant *Hizbollâh,* is run by members of the clergy and, in contrast to *Amal,* maintains close ties to Iran. It was founded in 1982 by then Iranian ambassador to Syria, Hâshemî Mohtashemî, who later became Iran's minister of the interior and opponent of President Rafsanjânî. The Hizbollâh follows a course committed to the ideas of Khomeinî, i.e., opposing Israel and spreading the Islamic revolution. The organization's secretary general, Shaykh Abbâs al-Mûsawî, and his wife were killed in 1992 in an Israeli attack. The spiritual leader of the Hizbollâh is Shaykh Muhammad Husayn Fadlallâh, of Beirut, who was born in 1934 in an-Najaf as the son of a Lebanese mujtahid.

The leading political role of the Shi'i clergy had different origins in Lebanon and Iraq than it did in Iran. In southern Lebanon and southern Iraq, the Shi'ites live in underdeveloped, rural areas. The clergy here are often the only people with a higher education and they are therefore predestined to take on the role of intellectual leader and pioneer. In addition, they maintain useful international connections. We recall that scholars from Lebanon played a major role in the sixteenth century in making Shi'ism the national religion in Iran. Quite a few Iranian mullah families are proud of their Arab-Lebanese heritage. The Shi'i ulamâ are also characterized by a high degree of mobility. The higher institutions of learning are located at the major shrines and pilgrimage sites, especially in an-Najaf, Karbalâ, Mashhad, and Qom, where ulamâ from throughout the world receive their education, study together, make friends, and often marry into local ulamâ families. The Shi'i ulamâ thus form a closely knit network, even beyond national borders.[41]

Social protest, political resistance, revolution, separatism, demands for a share of power, and efforts toward regional hegemony—all of this can be expressed through forms of Shi'i tradition. Religious traditions of the Shi'ites offer numerous patterns and models of suffering, rebellion, and self-sacrifice. These can easily be adapted to the times and, in comparison to conventional revolutionary ideologies of Western provenance, they do not only have the advantage of being comprehensible even to the traders at the bazaar or peasants in the smallest of villages, but for Shi'ites they are also something of their own, non-imported, that can be referred to in the struggle for justice—one of the fundamental principles of Islam. The promise of the return of the Hidden Imam who will establish a kingdom of justice on earth provides Shi'ism with a powerful utopia that can be instrumentalized for political mobilization.

Notes

PART ONE

1. Shaykh al-Mufîd, *Kitâb al-Irshâd. The Book of Guidance into the Lives of the Twelve Imams,* tr. I.K.A. Howard (Horsham and London, 1981), 4.
2. al-Mufîd, *Kitâb al-Irshâd,* 5.
3. The name means "thing with the spine." As we know from later descriptions, this is a double-edged sword with a ridge in the middle of the blade, hence the name. The iconography of later traditional Shi'i art changed the two cutting edges into two points, senseless in terms of weapon technology.
4. al-Mufîd, *Kitâb al-Irshâd,* 15.
5. Abû Mikhnaf's collection is cited by Sunni historians Balâdhurî, Dinawarî, and Tabarî, and Shi'i historians Ya'qûbî and al-Mufîd, *Kitâb al-Irshâd,* 296-379.
6. Abû Mikhnaf's work *The Book of Sulaymân ibn Surad* is apparently cited in its entirety in Tabarî's world chronicle from the tenth century (Tabarî, *Annales,* vol. VII: 497-513, 538-571).
7. David Pinault, *The Shiites,* 105f.; on the basis of numerous similar statements made by contemporary Shi'ites in Hyderabad, India, the author confirmed "a desire for collective atonement for their failure."
8. The epithet means "the splitter" or "opener." It is interpreted by Shi'ites as "opener of knowledge" *(Bâqir al-ilm).*
9. Mahmoud Ayoub, *Redemptive Suffering in Islam: A Study of the Devotional Aspects of "Ashura" in Twelver Shi'ism* (The Hague, 1978), 121ff. und 237ff.
10. Ayoub, *Redemptive Suffering,* 216, cited according to the collection of the Iranian al-Majlisî, *Bihâr al-anwâr,* LIII: 46.
11. al-Mufîd, *Kitâb al-Irshâd,* 541f., 548, 551-553.

PART TWO

1. Ehsan Yarshater, "Ta'ziyeh and Pre-Islamic Mourning Rites in Iran," in P. J. Chelkowski, ed., *Ta'ziyeh,* 88ff.; see also Heinz Halm, *Shiism,* tr. Janet Watson, (Edinburgh, 1991), 141-42.
2. Michael G. Morony, *Iraq After the Muslim Conquest* (Princeton, 1984), 451f., on self-sacrifice, see ibid., 475-77.
3. A. J. de Gobineau, *Trois ans en Asie* (Paris, 1980 [1905]), 324-327; ———, *Les religions et les philosophies dans l'Asie centrale,* 383; Roy Motta-

hedeh, *The Mantle of the Prophet* (New York, 1985), 170; Pinault, *The Shiites,* 131f.

4. Ibn al-Jawzî, *Muntazam* VII, 15, Ibn Taghrîbirdî, *Nujûm* (Cairo edition) III, 334.

5. Thomas Herbert, *A Relation of Some Yeares Travaile into Afrique, Asia, Indies* (London, 1634) [reprint Amsterdam, New York, 1971], 167.

6. Cited in Mottahedeh, *The Mantle of the Prophet* , 174-75.

7. Adam Olearius, *Vermehrte Moscowitische und Persianische Reisebeschreibung* (1656), 456ff. The first edition, *Newe Orientalische Reise,* was published in 1647.

8. Sinân ibn Anas killed Imam al-Husayn in Karbalâ with a lance, and Shimr or Shemr (actually *Shamir)* ibn Dhi'l-Jawshan beheaded him.

9. Persian *ajdar:* dragon.

10. Arabic *mesjid:* mosque.

11. *abdâl:* dervishes who perform as musicians at festivals.

12. Persian *mezâr:* cemetery. Shaykh Safî is the ancestor that the Safavid Dynasty is named after. Today, he is still honored as a saint in his mausoleum in Ardabîl.

13. Al-Abbâs, Mohammed's uncle, the forefather of the Baghdad Abbasid caliphate.

14. Arabic *naft:* pitch, tar, petroleum.

15. Most likely Persian *telâ,* the *"Golden One."*

16. E. Kaempfer, *Amoenitates Exoticae,* tr. W. Hinz, *Am Hofe des persischen Großkönigs* (Tübingen, 1977), 143.

17. William Francklin, *Observations made on a tour from Bengal to Persia in the years 1786-7* (London, 1790) [reprint Tehran, 1976], 239-254.

18. Here Francklin makes reference to traditional etymology that explains the Old Mesopotamian name Karbalâ as a compound deriving from the Arabic words *karb* (grief) and *belâ* (trial, affliction).

19. Arabic *minbar:* pulpit.

20. Persian *âkhûnd:* lower cleric, "parson"; *pîsh-namâz:* prayer leader.

21. Arabic *al-waq'a:* the battle.

22. Pinault, *The Shiites,* 56, 80 (note 4).

23. Arabic *khatîb:* preacher.

24. Persian *nakhl:* literally "garland." *Nakhl-e Moharram* or *nakhl-e mâtam* is used to refer to the coffins or tents carried in the processions, which are decorated with garlands.

25. Arabic *haydar:* lion; common epithet for Ali.

26. Adam Olearius, *Reisebeschreibung,* 434 ult.-436 paenult.

27. Pinaut, *The Shiites,* 89, 117.

28. Frédéric Maatouk, *La représentation de la mort de l'Imam Hussein à Nabatieh (Liban-Sud)* (Beirut, 1974); Ibrahim al-Haidari, *Zur Soziologie des schiitischen Chiliasmus. Ein Beitrag zur Erforschung des irakischen Passionsspiels,* Islamkundliche Untersuchungen, vol. 31 (Freiburg i.Br., 1975); Davoud Monchi-Zadeh, *Ta'ziya. Das persische Passionsspiel* (Stockholm, 1967); on Hyderabad, see the recent detailed information in

David Pinault, *The Shiites* (London, 1992).

29. James Morier, *A second journey through Persia, Armenia, and Asia Minor to Constantinople between the years 1810 and 1816* (London, 1818), 176-184.

30. Turkish *tekke,* Persian *takye,* originally meant "shelter," "tent," or "hut." It is used here for the provisional stage set up for the passion play; later it was used to connote a building for theater performances.

31. On the story of the martyrdom of the Byzantine ambassador, cf. William Francklin's report on p. 54-55, and de Gobineau's, p. 75, both in this book.

32. The Turkoman dynasty of the Qajar family ruled Iran from 1796 to 1925.

33. de Gobineau, *Trois ans en Asie* (Paris, 1905), 445-47.

34. A. J. de Gobineau, *Les Religions et les philosophies dans l'Asie centrale* (Paris, 1900), 359ff.

35. H. Brugsch, *Reise der K. Preussischen Gesandschaft nach Persien 1860 und 1861,* vol. II (Leipzig, 1863), 494.

36. J. Dieulafoy, *La Perse, la Chaldée et la Susiane* (Paris, 1887), 109, illus. p. 111.

37. Mottahedeh, *The Mantle of the Prophet,* 177-78.

38. de Gobineau, *Trois ans en Asie,* 447.

39. The well-known Shi'i theologian Muhammad ibn Bâbôye al-Qummi died in 991.

40. Monchi-Zadeh, *Ta'ziya. Das persische Passionsspiel,* 28.

41. Mottahedeh, *The Mantle of the Prophet,* 179.

42. de Gobineau, *Les Religions et les philosophies dans l'Asie centrale,* 376f.

43. Thomas Lyell, *The Ins and Outs of Mesopotamia* (London, 1923), 65: cited in Pinault, *The Shiites,* 111.

44. On this subject, see also Pinault, *The Shiites,* 109-112; 131f.

45. de Gobineau, *Les Religions et les philosophies dans l'Asie centrale,* 377f.

46. Pinault, *The Shiites,* 122.

47. Pinault, *The Shiites,* 110.

48. Pinault, *The Shiites,* 108.

49. W. Ende, "The Flagellations of Muharram and the Shi'ite Ulama," *Der Islam* 55 (1978), 19-36.

50. Pinault, *The Shiites,* 103-106.

51. On this subject, cf. Mottahedeh, *The Mantle of the Prophet,* 175

PART THREE

1. See also: A. Sachedina, "Al-Khums: The Fifth in the Imâmî Shî'î Legal System," in *Journal of Near Eastern Studies* 39 (1980), 275-289; N. Calder, "Khums in Imâmî Shî'î Jurisprudence, From the Tenth to the Sixteenth Century A.D.," in *Bulletin of the School of Oriental and African Studies* 45 (1982), 39-47.

2. Mottahedeh, 251-252, vividly describes the practice of collecting and distributing the *khums* at the Qom "court" of the popular Grand Âyatollâh Mar'ashi, who died in 1991.

3. Pinault, 93.

4. H. Halm, *The Empire of the Mahdi: The Rise of the Fatimids (875-973)*, tr. Michael Bonner (Leiden: E.J. Brill, 1996).

5. English edition: Shaykh Abu Ja'far al-Kulayni, *al-Kafi*, tr. Sayyid Muhammad Hasan Rizvi (Tehran, 1398/1978).

6. The Arabic titles are: *al-Istibsâr fîmâ 'khtulifa fîhi min al-akhbâr* and *Tahdhîb al-ahkâm.*

7. On the relevant passages of this book, *Mabâdi' al-wusûl ilâ ilm al-usûl (The points of departure from which knowledge of the principles is attained),* see Halm, *Shiism,* 68ff.

8. Allâma al-Hillî, *Mabâdi',* ed. 'Abd al-Husayn Muh, 'Alî (al-Baqqâl), (an-Najaf 1390/1970), 247.

9. This tension-filled relationship is treated in detail in: S.A. Arjomand, *The Shadow of God and the Hidden Imam* (Chicago, 1984).

10. Arjomand, *The Shadow of God,* 184f.; Halm, *Shiism,* 94ff.

11. Arjomand, *The Shadow of God,* 230f.

12. Kulaynî, *al-Kâfî,* I, 200.

13. Richard, 100; Mottahedeh, 242.

14. All these figures were made available by the secretary general *(dabîr)* of the "High Council of the Hawza," Âyatollâh Mo'men; April 1993.

15. The land reform act of 1962-63 did not affect those endowments *(auqâf,* singular *waqf)* whose proceeds served charitable purposes—schools, mosques, social facilities. It treated all foundations serving private interests *(waqf-e khâss)*, including certain sharîf or mullah families, as common real estate. Richard, 72-74; Mottahedeh, 244.

16. Jalâl Âl-e Ahmad, *Occidentosis: A Plague from the West,* with an introduction by Hamid Algar (Berkeley, 1984).

17. Mottadeheh, 287-336; cf. also Richard, 115ff.

18. Richard, 129.

19. Sharî'atî's main works that have been translated into English are *Red Shi'ism,* tr. Habib Shirazi (Tehran, 1979), and *Marxism and Other Western Fallacies* (Berkeley, 1980).

20. On Sharî'atî's life and works, cf. Richard, 126-139; Hamid Algar, *The Roots of the Islamic Revolution,* London 1983.

21. Ali Shariati, *Red Shi'ism* , 15.

22. Shariati, *Red Shi'ism* , 17, 23-24.

23. Richard, 95.

24. Cited in Mottahedeh, 302.

25. Ali Shariati, *Shahâdat* (Tehran, 1972), 104.

26. Shariati, *Red Shi'ism,* 14.

27. Shariati, *Red Shi'ism,* 12, 14-15.

28. M.M.J. Fischer, *Iran from Religious Dispute to Revolution* (Cambridge, MA, 1980); N.R. Keddie, *Roots of Revolution* (New Haven, CT and

London, 1981), with an essay by Y. Richard; H. Algar, *The Roots of the Islamic Revolution* (London, 1983); S. Bakhash, *The Reign of the Ayatollahs—Iran and the Islamic Revolution* (London, 1985); N.R. Keddie and E. Hooglund, eds., *The Iranian Revolution and the Islamic Republic* (Syracuse, NY, 1986); M.M. Milani, *The Making of Iran's Islamic Revolution: From Monarchy to Islamic Republic,* (Boulder, CO and London, 1988); S.A. Arjomand, *The Turban for the Crown: The Islamic Revolution in Iran* (Oxford, 1988); H. Amirahmade, *Revolution and Economic Transition: The Iranian Experience* (Albany, NY, 1990). The following works in German are notable: Y. Richard, *Die Geschichte der Schia in Iran* (Berlin, 1983); A. Taheri, *Chomeini und die Islamische Revolution* (Hamburg, 1985); D. Gholamasad, *Iran—Die Entstehung der "Islamischen Revolution"* (Hamburg, 1985). A concise analysis of the Iranian revolution is offered in P. Pawelka, *Der Vordere Orient und die Internationale Politik* (Stuttgart, 1993), 86-89.

29. Khomeinî, *Kashf al-asrâr* (Tehran, n.d.), 185.
30. A analysis of the book can be found in: Vanessa Martin, "Religion and State in Khumainî's Kashf al-Asrâr," in *Bulletin of the School of Oriental and African Studies* 56 (1993), 34-45.
31. See note 15 (part 3) above.
32. *Islam and Revolution: Writings and Declarations of Imam Khomeini,* trans. and annotated by Hamid Algar (Berkeley, 1981).
33. *Islam and Revolution*, 35, 36, 38-39 [Arabic edition: *al-Hukûma* (Beirut, 1979), 17-21].
34. Ibid., p. 31 (Arabic edition: *al-Hukûma,* 12).
35. Ibid., p. 42 (Arabic edition: *al-Hukûma,* 26).
36. Ibid., p. 64 (Arabic edition: *al-Hukûma,* 51f).
37. Ibid., p. 45 (Arabic edition: *al-Hukûma,* 29-31).
38. Cited in the newspaper: *Kayhan International* (22 April 1993), 12.
39. *The Proceedings of the Council to Reconsider the Constitution of the Islamic Republic of Iran* (Tehran, 1989), vol. 1, p. 174: Cited in: M. M. Milani, "The Transformation of the Velayat-e Faqîh Institution: From Khomeini to Khamenei," in: *The Muslim World* 82 (1992), 181.
40. Milani, 185f.
41. An informative survey of the family connections between the large Iraqi and Iranian ulamâ families is presented in the form of family trees in: Momen, *Introduction,* 132-134.

Bibliography

Adjami, Fouad, *The Vanished Imam: Musa al Sadr and the Shia of Lebanon* (London, 1986).

Akhavi, Shahrough, *Religion and Politics in Contemporary Iran: Clergy-State Relations in the Pahlavi Period* (Albany, NY, 1980).

Algar, Hamid, *Religion and State in Iran 1785-1906: The Role of the Ulama in the Qajar Period* (Berkeley and Los Angeles, CA, 1969).

Arjomand, Said Amir, *The Shadow of God and the Hidden Imam: Religion, Political Order, and Societal Change in Shi'ite Iran from the Beginning to 1890* (Chicago, 1984).

Ayoub, Mahmoud, *Redemptive Suffering in Islam: A Study of the Devotional Aspects of "Ashura" in Twelver Shi'ism* (The Hague, 1978).

Chelkowski, Peter J., ed., *Ta'ziyah: Ritual and Drama in Iran* (New York, 1979).

Cole, Juan R. I., and Nikki R. Keddie, eds., *Shi'ism and Social Protest* (New Haven, CT, 1986).

Halm, Heinz, *Shiism*, tr. Janet Watson (Edinburgh, 1991).

Kohlberg, Etan, *Belief and Law in Imami Shi'ism* (Hampshire and Brooksfield, 1991), *(Variorum Reprints,* collection of 17 essays).

Kramer, Martin, ed., *Shi'ism, Resistance, and Revolution* (London, 1987).

Momen, Moojan, *An Introduction to Shi'i Islam: The History and Doctrines of Twelver Shi'ism* (New Haven, CT, 1985).

Monchi-Zadeh, Davoud, *Ta'ziya: Das persische Passionsspiel* (Stockholm, 1967).

Morony, Michael G., *Iraq After the Muslim Conquest* (Princeton, 1984).

Mottahedeh, Roy, *The Mantle of the Prophet* (New York, 1985).

Müller, Hildegard, *Studien zum persischen Passionsspiel* (Freiburg i.Br., 1966).

Pinault, David, *The Shiites: Ritual and Popular Piety in a*

Muslim Community (London, 1992).

Pohl-Schöberlein, Monika, *Die schiitische Gemeinschaft des Südlibanon (Gabal 'Amil) innerhalb des libanesischen konfessionellen Systems* (Berlin, 1986).

Richard, Yann, *Die Geschichte der Schia in Iran. Grundlagen einer Religion* (Berlin, 1983).

Rieck, Andreas, *Die Schiiten und der Kampf um den Libanon. Politische Chronik 1958-1988*, Deutsches Orient-Institut Hamburg, Mitteilungen [Announcements], vol. 33 (1989).

Roemer, Hans Robert, *Persien auf dem Weg in die Neuzeit. Iranische Geschichte von 1350-1759* (Stuttgart and Beirut, 1989).

Sachedina, Abdulaziz A., *Islamic Messianism: The Idea of the Mahdi in Twelver Shi'ism* (Albany, NY, 1981).

————, *The Just Ruler (as-sultan al-'adil) in Shi'ite Islam: The Comprehensive Authority of the Jurist in Imamite Jurisprudence* (Oxford, 1988).

Schmidtke, Sabine, *The Theology of al-'Allama al-Hilli (died 726/1325)* (Berlin, 1991).

Shaykh al-Mufid, *Kitab al-Irshad: The Book of Guidance into the Lives of the Twelve Imams,* tr. I.K.A. Howard (Horsham and London, 1981).

Taheri, Amir, *Chomeini und die Islamische Revolution* (Hamburg, 1985).

Tellenbach, Silvia, *Untersuchungen zur Verfassung der Islamischen Republik Iran vom 15. November 1979* (Berlin, 1985).

Index